41610

510.28 Schwob, Pierre R
Sch
　　　How to use pocket
　　　calculators

WITHDRAWN

Urbandale Public Library
Urbandale, Iowa 50322

HOW TO USE POCKET CALCULATORS

PIERRE R. SCHWOB

PETROCELLI/CHARTER   NEW YORK 1976

Copyright Pierre R. Schwob 1976

All rights reserved. No part of this work covered by the copyrights hereon may be reproduced or used in any form or by any means—graphic, electronic, or mechanical, including photocopying, recording, or taping, or information storage and retrieval systems—without written permission of the publisher.

First Printing

Printed in the United States of America

To my father and
To my mother

AUTHOR'S NOTES

Abbreviations

Two frequently used abbreviations in this book will be:

RTR: Read the result on the display
WTR: Write the displayed answer for future use.

Negative Numbers

The generalized steps presented in this book are designed with the assumption that your calculator can accept a *negative number* as *factor* or *divisor* or that it offers a $\boxed{+/-}$ key. For instance, to solve $3 - (4 \times 6) =$ the following chain calculation is used:

$4 \boxed{\times} 6 \boxed{\times} \boxed{-} \boxed{1} \boxed{+} 3 \boxed{=}$ RTR: -21

Note that this problem is solved as if written

$$-(4 \times 6) + 3 = -21$$
$$\text{or } 3 + [(-1)(4 \times 6)] = -21$$

where we <u>multiply</u> the product of 4 and 6 <u>by −1 to get a negative term</u> that can, in turn, be added to 3.

The sequence

$$\boxed{\times}\ \boxed{-}\ \boxed{1}$$

is important in many calculations since it can convert a term from positive to negative and vice versa.

If your calculator offers the $\boxed{+/-}$ key, use it whenever the sequence $\boxed{\times}\ \boxed{-}\ \boxed{1}$ appears in a *generalized steps* procedure. For example, to solve the above problem, press in turn:

$$4\ \boxed{\times}\ 6\ \boxed{+/-}\ \boxed{+}\ 3\ \boxed{=} \qquad \text{RTR: } -21$$

If your calculator does not accept a negative number as factor or divisor and does not offer the $\boxed{+/-}$ key, there are three options:

1. If you feel secure with algebra, you can "cheat" and perform the following steps to solve the problem:

$$\boxed{C}\ \boxed{-}\ 4\ \boxed{\times}\ 6\ \boxed{+}\ 3\ \boxed{=} \qquad \text{RTR: } -21$$

This method, however, is not always possible and is dangerous.

2. If your algebra is too slim, you will have to solve the problem in two sequences:

First: $\quad 4\ \boxed{\times}\ 6\ \boxed{=} \qquad$ WTR: 24
Second: $\quad 3\ \boxed{-}\ 24\ \boxed{=} \qquad$ RTR: −21

Whenever the sequence $\boxed{\times}\ \boxed{-}\ \boxed{1}$ is present in a procedure, you will have to solve the part preceding $\boxed{\times}\ \boxed{-}\ \boxed{1}$ and note the result (press $\boxed{=}$ when you arrive at $\boxed{\times}\ \boxed{-}\ \boxed{1}$, and instead of it). Then press $\boxed{C}\ \boxed{-}$ and enter your written result before resuming your calculation, starting exactly after $\boxed{\times}\ \boxed{-}\ \boxed{1}$. If the simple sequence $\boxed{\times}\ \boxed{-}$ is

Author's Notes

found (notice that $\boxed{1}$ is absent this time), solve the part preceding $\boxed{\times}$ $\boxed{-}$ and write down the result. Then press $\boxed{C}$ $\boxed{-}$, enter your written result, press $\boxed{\times}$, and continue your calculation starting exactly after $\boxed{\times}$ $\boxed{-}$.

3. The third option, which is strongly recommended is to acquire a calculator that offers the feature in question.

CONTENTS

Author's Notes   vii

Preface   xv

PART ONE: LEARNING TO USE YOUR CALCULATOR   1

Chapter One: Introduction to Calculation   3
Calculator Keys   4
Entering a Number   5
The Operations   5
Chain Calculation   6
The Constant   6

Chapter Two: A Few Definitions   9
Different Kinds of Numbers   9
Symbols of Relationship   10
Repetitive Decimals   11
Subscripts   11
Reciprocals   12
Factorial   12

xi

Summation of Series 13
Product of Series 13

Chapter Three: How to Interpret Mathematical Formulas 15
Arithmetic Equations 15
Algebraic Equations 16
Symbols 18
Restructuring the Terms 26

PART TWO: SOLVING COMMON PROBLEMS 31

Chapter Four: The Rule of Three 33
Direct Variation 33
Inverse Variation 36

Chapter Five: Percentage 39
Markup 43
Discount 48
Multiple Trade Discount 49

Chapter Six: Conversions 51
Length Conversion 51
Area Conversion 53
Volume Conversion 55
Mass Conversion 56
Temperature Conversion 57

PART THREE: BANKING PROBLEMS 59

Chapter Seven: Simple Interest 61

Chapter Eight: Compound Interest 67

Chapter Nine: Discount to Yield 73

Chapter Ten: Annuities 77
Sinking Fund 77
Direct Reduction of a Loan 78

Contents

PART FOUR: STATISTICAL OPERATIONS   83

Chapter Eleven: The Means   85
Arithmetic Mean   85
Geometric Mean   86
Harmonic Mean   87
Median   88
Mode   88

Chapter Twelve: Linear Regression   89
Least Squares Method   89
Straight Line   92
Trend Line   96
Coefficient of Determination (r^2)   107

Chapter Thirteen: Probability   115
Simple Probability   116
Composed Probability   117
Permutation   120
Variation   122
Combination   124

PART FIVE: SCIENTIFIC NOTATION   127

Chapter Fourteen: Description of Scientific Notation   129

Chapter Fifteen: The Operations   133

Appendix A: Tables, Formulas, and Symbols   137

Appendix B: Series   143
Arithmetic Series   143
Geometric Series   144

Appendix C: Geometric Formulas   145
Plane Geometry   145
Solid Geometry   145

Index   153

PREFACE

In a few short years the pocket calculator has gone from a relatively expensive tool of specialists to a mass-produced consumer item that is priced within the reach of almost everyone. These calculators are not toys; they can solve complicated problems at the flick of a few buttons. Unfortunately, all too often the proud owner of a new calculator does not really know how to use it. The mathematical skill that is required to get the most out of these little brains is, indeed, not widespread. This is what this book is all about.

This book has been designed with the following in mind: First, it is based on the assumption that the reader will operate a calculator with the following standard features: four functions ($+$, $-$, $\times$, $\div$), floating decimal point, automatic constant, and algebraic logic. Second, it is also assumed that no special knowledge of mathematics or algebra should be necessary to comprehend its content. Indeed the first chapters are devoted to a review of the basic knowledge necessary to avoid the layman's frustration in following such topics.

The material is grouped in five parts, each related to a particular type of problem. After the review of the basic techniques, the book offers a logical approach to the solution of percentages, banking and financial problems, conversions, probability and statistical calculation. Toward the end of this volume, the mathematically inclined reader will find various tables and formulas that might prove helpful for the computation of linear regression, geometric problems, and other algebraic sentences. A special chapter is devoted to the scientific notation that allows the handling of very large numbers or very small fractions on a standard eight-digit calculator.

Throughout the whole book, emphasis has been placed on ways to find the shortest route to the correct solution, that is to say, a demonstration of the use of the minimum number of steps in the resolution of any given problem. It is indeed the contention of the author that it is only in this manner that the pragmatic use of a calculator can come close to an art.

Although it is not possible to mention all collaborators by name, the assistance of the following individuals is acknowledged: O. Petrocelli, J. Tonero, L. Burton, R. Chlupsa, G. Jacobs, R. La Barbera, A. Schaeffer, and finally, but not least, gratitude is expressed to my father, who invited me to stay at his home in Switzerland where the major part of this manuscript was written.

Pierre R. Schwob
New York, December 1975

PART ONE
LEARNING TO USE YOUR CALCULATOR

CHAPTER 1

INTRODUCTION TO CALCULATION

First let us review the different keys and the basic operations that one can perform on a common calculator. The layout of this book is based on the assumption that you will operate a simple calculator offering the following features:

Addition ⎫
Subtraction ⎬ FUNCTIONS
Multiplication ⎪
Division ⎭
Floating decimal point
Automatic constant
Algebraic entry notation

There are two types of modes to enter numbers and functions in a calculator: *algebraic entry notation* and *reverse Polish notation.*

With the algebraic entry notation (or algebraic logic), you enter the numbers and functions as you would write them.

Example: Assuming we wanted to multiply 3 by 5, we would write $3 \times 5 =$ and then perform the following steps:

$$\boxed{3}\ \boxed{\times}\ \boxed{5}\ \boxed{=}$$

and thus read the result (15) on the display.

3

If, on the other hand, the calculator were programmed with the *reverse Polish notation*, you would press the following keys:

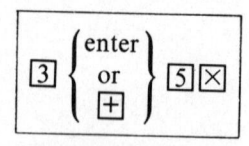

$$\boxed{3} \left\{ \begin{array}{c} \text{enter} \\ \text{or} \\ \boxed{+} \end{array} \right\} \boxed{5} \boxed{\times}$$

and read the result (15) on display.

Note that the function $\boxed{\times}$ is entered after the last number and that no $\boxed{=}$ key is used. This method reduces the number of steps needed for computing long and tedious equations, but it is rarely found in common calculators.

Some calculators with *mixed entry notation* are also manufactured. These use the *algebraic entry* for multiplication and division and the *reverse Polish* for the other functions. This system is confusing, and I would advise against it.

CALCULATOR KEYS

$\boxed{0}\boxed{1}\boxed{2}\boxed{3}\boxed{4}\boxed{5}\boxed{6}\boxed{7}\boxed{8}\boxed{9}$ are the *number entry* keys

$\boxed{.}$ is the *decimal point* key

$\boxed{+}\boxed{-}\boxed{\times}\boxed{\div}$ are the *function* keys

$\boxed{=}$ is the *equal sign* key or *terminal* key

$\boxed{C}$ or $\boxed{CE}$ or $\boxed{CL}$ are the *cancel* and *clear* keys, which are used to correct an erroneous entry or to clear the content of the calculator.[†]

[†] On some calculators there are two keys for these functions (clear/cancel), while on others one key performs both.

ENTERING A NUMBER

To enter a number, simply read that number from left to right and depress the corresponding keys in turn. When a decimal point is involved, just insert the *decimal point* key at its proper place in the sequence.

Example: To enter 3749.35 press, in turn:

$$\boxed{3}\ \boxed{7}\ \boxed{4}\ \boxed{9}\ \boxed{\cdot}\ \boxed{3}\ \boxed{5}$$

If there is only a zero to the left of the decimal point, just start with the $\boxed{\cdot}$ key; the depression of the $\boxed{0}$ key is unnecessary.

Example: To enter 0.618034 press, in turn:

$$\boxed{\cdot}\ \boxed{6}\ \boxed{1}\ \boxed{8}\ \boxed{0}\ \boxed{3}\ \boxed{4}$$

The calculator will automatically insert the *zero* to the left of the decimal point. Isn't that why you bought the calculator in the first place—to save time?

The same principle applies when there are no figures after the decimal point. *Example:* To enter 1975.00 press, in turn:

$$\boxed{1}\ \boxed{9}\ \boxed{7}\ \boxed{5}$$

The calculator does the rest!

THE OPERATIONS

A few short examples will illustrate the use of the function keys.

Add 5 to 3	$\boxed{3}\ \boxed{+}\ \boxed{5}\ \boxed{=}$	RTR: 8
Subtract 3 from 5	$\boxed{5}\ \boxed{-}\ \boxed{3}\ \boxed{=}$	RTR: 2
Multiply 5 times 3	$\boxed{5}\ \boxed{\times}\ \boxed{3}\ \boxed{=}$	RTR: 15
Divide 5 by 3	$\boxed{5}\ \boxed{\div}\ \boxed{3}\ \boxed{=}$	RTR: 1.6[†]

[†] (See p. 11) The last figure on the right will be 6 instead of 7 if your calculator doesn't perform an automatic roundoff.

CHAIN CALCULATION

To find the result of $[(5 + 3)2]/4$ (see p. 22), add 5 and 3, multiply the result by 2, and finally divide the last result by 4. But instead of doing it the long way—$5 + 3 = 8$; $8 \times 2 = 16$; $16 \div 4 = 4$—which requires a minimum of ten steps, you can perform a *chain calculation* that in this case requires only eight steps:

[5] [+] [3] [×] [2] [÷] [4] [=]   RTR: 4

You will notice that we use the [=] key only once at the end of our calculation and that no intermediate results have to be reentered or noted on a scratch pad.

The difference in number of steps increases in proportion to the complexity of the equation you want to solve. With a little practice and the help of the next chapter you will be able to "read" equations without any trouble and use the most elegant method—or minimum number of steps—to solve a problem.

THE CONSTANT

The constant feature allows the multiplication or division of different numbers by the same number (called *Constant*) without the reentry of the latter. (On most calculators the constant is usable on all four functions.) *Example:* Multiply 5, 20, 3.5 times 4.25

NOTE: Since the mode of entry of a constant varies with each manufacturer, the reader should carefully study the instructions delivered with the calculator.

To multiply the first number (5), execute

[4] [.] [2] [5] [×] [5] [=]   RTR: 21.25

Learning to Use Your Calculator

The "times 4.25" is now in the calculator's memory (constant). The next number to be multiplied (20) is then simply entered and multiplied with

$$\boxed{2}\ \boxed{0}\ \boxed{=}\qquad \text{RTR: 85}$$

The same thing for the last number (3.5):

$$\boxed{3}\ \boxed{\cdot}\ \boxed{5}\ \boxed{=}\qquad \text{RTR: 14.875}$$

Again, the mode of entry of a constant varies with each manufacturer. In these examples I assume that the number entered *before* the $\boxed{\times}$ key is accepted by the calculator as the constant (4.25). It is possible, however, that your calculator "remembers" the number entered *after* the $\boxed{\times}$ key, in which case the first multiplication will have to be reversed and entered as follows:

$$\boxed{5}\ \boxed{\times}\ \boxed{4}\ \boxed{\cdot}\ \boxed{2}\ \boxed{5}\ \boxed{=}$$

in order to program the correct constant. In any case the subsequent operations on the last two numbers (20 and 3.5) will follow the same steps described above.

The constant is also very useful when you want to *raise a number to a power*. To raise any number (N) to any power (P), means that P N's are multiplied together. This is written N^P (the P above the line is called the *exponent* and indicates the number of N's to be multiplied together). Don't be afraid of this strange notation; a few examples will convince you that it is, in fact, quite simple.

Example: Raise 2 to its sixth power ... or solve 2^6. Thus, multiply six 2's together: $2\times2\times2\times2\times2\times2 = 2^6 = 64$. Let's see how we can use the *constant* to solve the last example. First, press

$$\boxed{2}\ \boxed{\times}\ \boxed{2}$$

Now the "times 2" is in the calculator. Then simply press the $=$ key P minus 1 times, since we have already multiplied 2 by itself once by pressing 2 $\times$ 2. Since in this case $P = 6$, we have to press the equal sign key five times (indeed, $6 - 1 = 5$). Thus,

$$= \quad = \quad = \quad = \quad = \qquad \text{RTR: } 64$$

Example: Solve 1.02^3. Press:

$$1.02 \; \times \; 1.02 \; = \; = \qquad \text{RTR: } 1.061208$$

We pressed the $=$ key twice, since $3 - 1 = 2$.

With most calculators one is able to raise a number N to a power P simply by entering the number N *once,* by pressing the $\times$ key *once,* and then pressing the $=$ key $P - 1$ times. *Example:* 6.712^6.

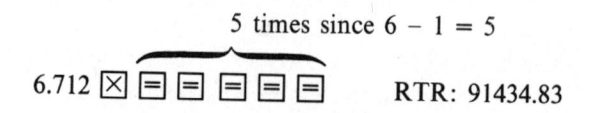

$$\overbrace{}^{\text{5 times since } 6 - 1 = 5}$$
$$6.712 \; \times \; = \; = \; = \; = \; = \qquad \text{RTR: } 91434.83$$

This is the method we shall use in this book since it is accepted by most calculators.

CHAPTER 2

A FEW DEFINITIONS

This chapter presents a few terms, definitions, and symbols we shall encounter in the text.

DIFFERENT KINDS OF NUMBERS

Arithmetic is the study of fundamental operations with real numbers. The set of *real numbers* is composed of the set of *rational numbers* and the set of *irrational numbers*.

Irrational numbers are real numbers that *cannot* be expressed in the form p/q where p and q are integers. That is,

$$\sqrt{2};\ \sqrt{3};\ \sqrt{1/2};\ \pi\ (\text{Pi});\ e;\ \ldots$$

The set of *rational numbers* is composed of the set of *integers* and the set of *fractional numbers*.

Fractional numbers are rational numbers that can be expressed in the form p/q where p and q are integers and where $1 \neq q \neq 0$ (which means that q cannot be equal to 1 or 0). That is,

$$\frac{5}{2};\ \frac{3}{4};\ \frac{1}{6};\ \frac{15}{16};\ 0.25;\ 9.2;\ 4\tfrac{1}{2};\ 1.\underline{1};\ \ldots$$

The set of *integers* is composed of the set of the *positive integers* (also called *natural numbers* or *counting numbers*), that is, 1, 2, 3, 4, ... (where the three dots mean "and so on"; the set of the *negative integers*, that is, ..., −4, −3, −2, −1; and the *empty set* or *zero* (0). Graphically:

```
                    COMPLEX NUMBERS
                   ⏞‾‾‾‾‾‾‾‾‾‾‾‾‾‾‾‾‾‾‾‾‾
    REAL NUMBERS              IMAGINARY NUMBERS
   ⏞‾‾‾‾‾‾‾‾‾‾‾‾‾‾‾‾‾‾
IRRATIONAL NUMBERS        RATIONAL NUMBERS
                         ⏞‾‾‾‾‾‾‾‾‾‾‾‾‾‾‾‾‾‾‾
                 INTEGERS          FRACTIONAL
                                    NUMBERS
                ⏞‾‾‾‾‾‾‾‾‾‾
NEGATIVE INTEGERS  |  POSITIVE INTEGERS
             ZERO          or
                       NATURAL NUMBERS
                           or
                       COUNTING NUMBERS
```

SYMBOLS OF RELATIONSHIP

$a = b$	means	a is *equal to* b
$a \neq b$	means	a is *not equal to* b
$a > b$	means	a is *greater than* b
$a < b$	means	a is *less than* b
$a \geq b$	means	a is *greater than or equal to* b
$a \leq b$	means	a is *less than or equal to* b
$a \simeq b$	means	a is *approximately equal to* b

Learning to Use Your Calculator

That is,

$$5 = \frac{5}{1} \qquad\qquad 5 \neq \frac{5}{2}$$

$$5 > 4 \qquad\qquad 5 < 6$$

$$e \simeq 2.718281828 \qquad \begin{array}{c} -1 < 0 < 1 \\ 5 < 6 > 4 \\ 4 > 3 < 5 \\ 5 > 4 > 3 \end{array} \qquad \pi \simeq 3.141592654$$

$$\sqrt{2} \simeq 1.414213562$$

REPETITIVE DECIMALS

A bar below a decimal figure or group of figures means that this figure or group of figures repeats itself infinitely.

$$\frac{1}{3} = 0.\underline{3} = 0.33333333333333333333 \ldots$$

$$\frac{5}{7} = 0.\underline{714285} = 0.714285714285714285 \ldots$$

$$\frac{5}{3} = 1.\underline{6} = 1.6666666666666 \ldots$$

$$\frac{52}{11} = 4.\underline{72} = 4.7272727272 \ldots$$

$$\frac{50}{7} = 7.\underline{142857} = 7.142857142857142857 \ldots$$

$$\frac{13}{6} = 2.1\underline{6} = 2.16666666666 \ldots$$

SUBSCRIPTS

A little number on the lower right side of a number is a *subscript*, which indicates a rank or the place this number has in a series.

$$a_1, a_2, a_3, a_4, a_5 \ldots a_n$$

where a_1 is the first number, a_2 is the second number, and a_n, by tradition, indicates the *last number*. This means that there are n numbers in the series.

RECIPROCALS

The *reciprocal* of a number is the quotient of 1 divided by this number.

$$\text{Reciprocal of } 5 = \frac{1}{5} = 0.2$$

$$\text{Reciprocal of } 0.25 = \frac{1}{0.25} = (1 \div 0.25) = 4$$

$$\text{Reciprocal of } -3 = \frac{1}{-3} = -0.\underline{3} = -0.33333333 \ldots$$

On most calculators with an automatic constant it is possible to obtain the reciprocal of a number by
    1. entering this number
    2. depressing ÷ once
    3. depressing = twice

FACTORIAL

The symbol $n!$ is read *factorial n* and denotes the products of the positive integers from 1 to n inclusive: $1! = 1$; $2! = 1 \times 2 = 2$; $3! = 1 \times 2 \times 3 = 6$; $4! = 1 \times 2 \times 3 \times 4 = 24$; and so on. (By definition: $0! = 1$.)

SUMMATION OF SERIES

Consider a series of numbers a_1, a_2, a_3, a_4; (here $n = 4$). Σa (read Sigma a) is then the sum of all a's. If $a_1 = 3$, $a_2 = 5$, $a_3 = 2$, and $a_4 = 3.4$, then $\Sigma a = 13.4$

PRODUCT OF SERIES

Consider a series of numbers a_1, a_2, a_3, a_4. Πa (read Pi a) is then the product of all a's.

If $a_1 = 3$, $a_2 = 5$, $a_3 = 2$, and $a_4 = 3.4$, then $\Pi a = 102$. Here Π is a capital letter as opposed to the lower-case π, which is equal to approximately 3.1416.

CHAPTER 3

HOW TO INTERPRET MATHEMATICAL FORMULAS

This chapter contains the basic knowledge necessary in "reading" a formula and using its "givens" on a calculator. A formula is an equation used to solve a specific problem. We can separate mathematical equations in two very general classes:
  1. The *ARITHMETIC* equations
  2. The *ALGEBRAIC* equations.

ARITHMETIC EQUATIONS

In arithmetic the numbers in an equation are always *known* quantities. A typical problem is to convert a known number of hours and minutes to minutes. *Example:* Convert 4 hours and 15 minutes to minutes. Since we know that there are 60 minutes in an hour, the problem is solved with $4 \times 60 + 15$, with a result of 255. The equation is thus written $4 \times 60 + 15 = 255$; or to be precise, $(4 \times 60) + 15 = 255$. This indicates that *first* one should multiply 4 by 60, and *then* add 15 to the result (240) to find 255.

Otherwise, a less alert reader might first add 15 to 60, and then multiply the result (900) by 4, which would yield the incorrect result of 3600. Indeed 3600 minutes would equal 60 hours!

We shall come back to this notation, called *aggregation*, later.

ALGEBRAIC EQUATIONS

In algebra some of the numbers in an equation may be known (they usually are called *constants*), but others are either unknown (they are the *unknowns*) or not specified (these are the *variables*).

The *unknowns* and the *variables* are represented by letters. Usually the variables are represented by letters from the beginning of the alphabet (a, b, c, ...) and the unknowns by letters borrowed from the end of the alphabet (... , x, y, z). More specifically, when there is only one unknown in the equation, the letter x is used.

The same problem of conversion stated above would be written as an algebraic equation $60a + b = x$, where a is *any* number of hours, b is *any* number of minutes, and x is the result, the unknown number of minutes.

In this equation, a and b are the *variables*; 60 is a *constant* and x is the *unknown*. Note that when a and b acquire different values, x will yield different answers. Indeed, if $a = 3$ and $b = 20$, x will be 200; if $a = 5$ and $b = 30$, x will be 330; and so on. Thus,

$$60a + b = x$$
$$a = \text{hours}; b = \text{minutes}; x = \text{minutes}$$

has become a *general formula* to convert hours and minutes to minutes.

This is precisely why algebra is used: to construct general formulas to solve specific problems in which the quantities can assume any value. The equation is in fact a "how to" or "instruction manual" that one follows to solve a specific problem where the numbers (variables) can be different every time.

Learning to Use Your Calculator 17

The formula

$$60a + b = x$$

is read as follows: To solve x (to convert a number of hours and minutes to minutes), first multiply a (the number of hours, a variable) by 60 (a constant), and then add b (the number of minutes, another variable) to the previous result.

An algebraic equation or formula used to solve a problem should always be accompanied by a description of the letters in order to follow its "instructions" easily. The following is meaningless:

$$\frac{\pi \cdot 2 \cdot a}{86400 \cdot b} = x$$

The following, however, is complete:

$$\frac{\pi \cdot 2 \cdot a}{86400 \cdot b} = x$$

where a = average distance of a planet to its sun in miles
b = number of days (of 24 hours) for this planet to complete a revolution around its sun
x = orbital speed of the planet in miles per second

It gives all the information one needs to determine at what speed the Earth, for example, orbits around the sun. Since $a \simeq 93$ million miles and $b \simeq 365$ days (one year) we have

$$\frac{\pi \cdot 2 \cdot 93000000}{86400 \cdot 365} \simeq 18.5 \text{ miles per second}$$

You know that $\pi \simeq 3.14159$. In this case, the equation gives the following instructions:
1. Multiply a by 2.
2. Multiply the result by π (Pi).
3. Multiply b by 86400 (the number of seconds in a 24-hour day).

4. Divide the result found in (2) by the result found in (3). Now, unless you are working with a sophisticated calculator, you will have already reached an *overflow* after your first step (93000000 × 2 yields an answer of 9 digits). You can circumvent that kind of difficulty by rearranging the steps. For example:
 1. Divide *a* by 86400.
 2. Multiply the result by 2.
 3. Multiply the result found in (2) by π (Pi).
 4. Divide the last result by *b*.

You are performing a simple chain calculation described in the previous chapter:

93000000 ÷ 86400 × 2 × 3.14159 ÷ 365 =   RTR: 18.529

You are thus able to reach the answer without any difficulty. We will return to this "restructuring" later.

SYMBOLS

In defining various symbols one may encounter in an equation, we will limit ourselves to the material needed for the understanding of this book.

Symbols of Functions

We have already seen that the letters are either *variables* or *unknowns* and that the defined numbers are the *constants*. These (algebraic) numbers (defined or not) are related by *functions*, which determine the operation that is to be performed between two (or more) numbers.

Addition is signified by the sign +; 5 + 2 = 17 and *a* + *b* = *c* where 5, 12, *a*, *b*, are the *terms* of the addition and where 17 and *c* its *sum*.

Learning to Use Your Calculator

Subtraction is signified by the sign $-$; $17 - 9 = 8$ and $a - b = c$ where 17 and a are the *minuend*, 9 and b the *subtrahend*, and 8 and c the *difference*.

Multiplication can be signified in various ways. In arithmetic, the sign $\times$ is generally used; $5 \times 4 = 20$ where 5 and 4 are the *factors* and 20 is the *product*. In algebra the $\times$ could be misunderstood for the letter X so one uses either a dot—$a \cdot b = c$ where a and b are the factors and c the product—or, more usually, no sign at all: ab means a multiplied by b (as in $ab = c$); $a(b + c) = d$ means a multiplied by the sum of b and c is equal to d; $16a$ means sixteen a's or, which is equivalent, sixteen times a.

Division can also be signified in various ways; $\div$ or : or, more usually, the *bar of fraction*—$a \div b = c$ or $a : b = c$ where a is the *dividend*, b is the *divisor*, and c is the *quotient*. More usually, $a/b = c$, which also means a divided by b is equal to c, where a is the *numerator*, b is the *denominator*, and c is the *quotient*.

It is important to remember that every fraction indicates a division: $20/5 = 4$ and $1/4$ is equal to 0.25. To convert the *rational number* that is in the form of a *fraction* $7/8$ to a *decimal fraction*, on your calculator, simply press

$$7 \; \boxed{\div} \; 8 \; \boxed{=} \qquad \text{RTR:} \quad 0.875$$

Hence, when you read in your newspaper that a stock was traded at $116\,\tfrac{7}{8}$, it means that its price was $\$116.875$.

Here is, one should point out, one of the idiosyncrasies of mathematical notation. As we said before, when there is no function sign between two numbers, it is understood that they are to be multiplied together. Indeed, $a\tfrac{b}{c}$ is equivalent to a times the quotient of b divided by c. But when one writes a fraction, in arithmetic, it is understood that $116\,\tfrac{7}{8}$ is equivalent to $116 + \tfrac{7}{8}$ or, in other words, 116 plus the quotient of 7 divided by 8. Obviously, $116\,\tfrac{7}{8}$ is not equal to 101.50.

The "nth" power of a is signified by $a^n = b$ where a is the *base*, and n is the *exponent*, and b is the nth power of a. $5^2 = 5 \times 5 = 25$; $3^4 = 3 \times 3 \times 3 \times 3 = 81$ (See the section concerning the constant on p. 7.)

The "nth" root of a is signified by $\sqrt[n]{a} = r$ where a is the *base* (or *radicand*), n is the *index of the radical* (signed integer), and r is the nth root of a (or *radical*) (where a is the nth power of r).

$$\sqrt[2]{25} = 5 \text{ (Indeed, } 5^2 = 25.)$$
$$\sqrt[4]{81} = 3 \text{ (Indeed, } 3^4 = 81.)$$

As subtraction is the inverse of addition and division the inverse of multiplication, the nth root of a is the inverse operation of the nth power of a.

Another idiosyncracy is that when n (the index of the radical) is not mentioned, one understands that we have to find the second (or square) root of the base a. $\sqrt{25} = \sqrt[2]{25} = 5$. When you see a notation such as $\sqrt[3]{64}$ you should ask yourself what three same numbers multiplied by themselves give 64 (r • r • r = 64)? This can be solved (the index must be an integer) on an ordinary calculator with what is called an *algorithm* or *iterative solution*.

An *algorithm* is a series of operations one performs several times until the answers yielded at the end of two consecutive series are identical or until a given result is reached. The following steps can solve any root as long as the index is an integer. (If the index is a fractional or irrational number, one has to use *logarithms*, an explanation of which is beyond the scope of this book.) Solve for the nth root of base a or $\sqrt[n]{a} = r$:

1. First, take a guess (you can be far off, it doesn't really matter) as to the value of r.
2. Then divide the base n minus one times by the guess (n is the index).
3. Add the guess n minus one times to the previous result.
4. Divide this result by the index n.
5. Go back to step (1) and use the final result in place of your initial guess.

Learning to Use Your Calculator

6. Repeat these steps until the result yielded in step (4) is the same twice. This will be your answer (r).

Take as an example finding the cubic root of 64. In other words, solve $\sqrt[3]{64}$.

1. First, take a guess; let's say 5.
2. 64 ÷ 5 = 12.8
   12.8 ÷ 5 = 2.56 } twice since "3 minus one" equals 2
3. 2.56 + 5 = 7.56
   7.56 + 5 = 12.56 } ditto
4. 12.56 ÷ 3 = 4.18$\underline{6}$
5. 4.18$\underline{6}$ becomes your new guess.
6. Go back to step 1.

1. With 4.18$\underline{6}$ as our guess we perform:
2. 64 ÷ 4.18$\underline{6}$ = 15.286624
   15.286624 ÷ 4.18$\underline{6}$ = 3.6512637
3. 3.6512637 + 4.18$\underline{6}$ = 7.8379303
   7.8379303 + 4.18$\underline{6}$ = 12.024596
4. 12.04596 ÷ 3 = 4.0081986
5. 4.0081986 becomes your new guess.
6. Go back to step (1).

In the next sequence we try again with 4.0081986 in place of the last guess ... and so on ... until the same result is yielded twice at the end of step 4. In this case it will be 4 (or 3.$\underline{9}$). Here again we can make good use of the constant. To compute any root you will need to enter the guess and then the corrected guesses only twice in each series. (If your calculator has an independent memory, this computation will become a simple chain calculation.)

Generalized Steps: Root Calculation

1. TAKE A GUESS FOR r (an estimate of the answer).
2. BASE ÷ GUESS = (Depress = n minus one times; i.e., $\sqrt[4]{\text{base}}$, depress = 3 times; $\sqrt[9]{\text{base}}$, depress = 8 times)
3. + GUESS = (same remark as in step 2)
4. ÷ INDEX =

5. WRITE THE ANSWER yielded in step 4 = new guess
6. GO TO STEP 2 using the new guess and repeat the series of steps (2 to 5) until the ANSWER at step 5 is identical twice.

Example: Solve $\sqrt[5]{40}$
1. Guess: 3
2. 40 ÷ 3 = = = =   (four times since 5 minus one is 4)
3. ÷ 3 = = = =   (ditto)
4. ÷ 5 =
5. We write the answer: 2.4987654 = new guess
6. We go to step 2 again.

2. 40 ÷ 2.4987654 = = = =
3. ÷ 2.4987654 = = = =
4. ÷ 5 =
5. WTR: 2.2042172
6. We go to step 2 again.

2. 40 ÷ 2.2042172 = = = =
3. ÷ 2.2042172 = = = =
4. ÷ 5 =
5. WTR: 2.1022744
6. We go to step 2 ... and here are the results you'll get at the next steps (5): 2.0913934; 2.091279; 2.091279. Thus the answer is 2.091279. Indeed, 2.091279 × = = = = is 39.999987 ≃ 40, which is the closest you'll get on an eight-digit calculator.

Symbols of Aggregation

As explained at the beginning of this chapter, it is sometimes necessary to group a series of numbers and the functions relating them in an equation. We wrote 4 × 60 + 15 and then added parentheses—(4 × 60) + 15—to indicate that we should first multiply 4 by 60 and only then add 15 to the result of the multiplication.

Parentheses are symbols of aggregation. Other symbols are

Learning to Use Your Calculator 23

brackets [ ] and *braces* { }. These symbols are introduced to designate groups of terms† that should be treated as one quantity. In order of priority, parentheses are usually used within brackets, and brackets within braces: − { −5[6 − 7(9 − 10)] + 3} = 62. The *rules of signs* are necessary if your calculator doesn't accept a negative number as the factor of a multiplication (or division) or doesn't offer the key [+/−] , which allows changing the sign (from plus to minus and vice versa) of the displayed number. Try to depress the following keys:

[−] [5] [×] [−] [3] [=]

If the displayed answer is 15, it is very probable that your calculator "knows" these rules and will apply them automatically. The majority of the calculators on the market have this capacity. If you own another type of calculator, you will have to memorize the following and apply it yourself, or follow the instructions delivered with your calculator. In any case, remember to depress the Cancel key before such operations.

When two numbers have the same sign (both + or both −), their product (or quotient) will be positive.†† When two numbers have opposite signs (one +, the other −), their product (or quotient) will be negative. Another important rule is that when a minus sign is in front of a quantity (to the left of an aggregation or an algebraic term), this quantity is de facto multiplied by − 1 (negative one). Thus, − (7 + 3) is equivalent to (− 1)(7 + 3); hence − (7 + 3) is equivalent to − 10; On your calculator depress:

[7] [+] [3] [×] [−] [1] [=]   RTR: − 10

†An algebraic term is the *product* or *quotient* of one or more general numbers and of a *numerical factor* (which can be any natural number) with a prefixed sign. (The + sign used to indicate a positive number is frequently omitted): $2a$; $3X^2$; $2\sqrt{5}$; $-7bX$; $-5b/-a$; and so on.

††This explains why the square root (or any even root) of a negative number cannot be a real number. Indeed, if $\sqrt{a} = r$, r multiplied by itself once gives a. Since r is multiplied by itself, the product a will always be positive. The answer to $\sqrt{-a}$ is called an *imaginary number*.

(The sequence ☒ ⊟ ☐ can be replaced by the depression of a ⊞ key, if available.) Remember that when a number or a quantity has no sign to its left, it is understood that it is a positive number or positive quantity.

To solve an equation containing symbols of aggregation one should "remove" them one by one, starting with the innermost symbols and terminating with the outermost symbols. We shall demonstrate such "removal" in solving the last example: $-\{-5[6 - 7(9 - 10)] + 3\}$

The first step is to eliminate the parentheses. To do so, we have to perform the operation within them and the multiplication directly without them. Remember that an algebraic number and its factor are the elements of a term, and the latter has to be considered as one quantity. Thus, we solve $7(9 - 10) = 7(-1) = -7$. (Remember the rule of signs.) We have $-\{-5[6 - (-7)] + 3\}$

We solve the quantity within the brackets and its factor, $-5[6 - (-7)] = -5(13) = -65$. (Remember that $-(-7) = +7$; thus, $6 - (-7) = +13 = 13$.) We have $-\{-65 + 3\}$ and finally solve with $-\{-65 + 3\} = -(-62) = +62 = 62$.

You would perform the following chain calculation on your calculator:

⑨ ⊟ ① ⓪ ☒ ⊟ ⑦ ⊞ ⑥ ☒ ⊟ ⑤ ⊞ ③ ☒ ⊟ ① ⊟
RTR: 62

Another example is $-\left\{-5\left[\dfrac{-(3+3)}{2}\right]-5\right\}$.

1. Add 3 to 3.
2. Multiply the sum by -1.
3. Divide the product by 2.
4. Multiply the quotient by -5.
5. Subtract 5 from the product.
6. Multiply the difference by -1.

With your calculator:

Learning to Use Your Calculator 25

$\boxed{3}\boxed{+}\boxed{3}\boxed{\times}\boxed{-}\boxed{1}\boxed{\div}\boxed{2}\boxed{\times}\boxed{-}\boxed{5}\boxed{-}\boxed{5}\boxed{\times}\boxed{-}\boxed{1}\boxed{=}$

RTR: − 10

Unfortunately, it is not always possible to solve an equation on a common calculator without writing down intermediate results. (A memory is of great help in these cases; even better, a calculator with a *four-registers stack*, such as one of the Hewlett-Packard products that use the RPN Logic (Reverse Polish Notation), will allow you to solve the most complex equations without any trouble.)

With a common calculator, an equation such as [10(15 + 17)]/[21 + 43] has to be solved in two steps. A first calculation will "treat" the denominator:

$\boxed{2}\boxed{1}\boxed{+}\boxed{4}\boxed{3}\boxed{=}$ WTR: 64

We can now solve with:

$\boxed{1}\boxed{5}\boxed{+}\boxed{1}\boxed{7}\boxed{\times}\boxed{1}\boxed{0}\boxed{\div}\boxed{6}\boxed{4}\boxed{=}$ RTR: 5

where the denominator (intermediate result 64) has been entered at its proper place in the sequence. You will note that we chose to calculate the denominator first as the intermediate result instead of the numerator. This was done to save steps. Had we chosen to calculate the numerator first, we would have had to write down its value, then compute the denominator, jotting down this second intermediate result before performing the ultimate division.

It is always preferable to choose the most "elegant" methods in solving problems—that is, methods involving the minimum number of steps allowed by the machine in use. In this manner the pragmatic use of a calculator can come close to an art!

In the context of the aggregation let us solve an equation

involving a quantity raised to a power and demonstrate once more the shortest method of finding its value. Solve $[2 + 3(4 + 5)^5]/7$. Remember that a quantity raised to a power and also multiplied by a factor (in this case the quantity is $4 + 5$, the power—or exponent—is 5 and the factor is 3) has to be first raised to its power and only then multiplied by its factor. Thus:
 1. Add 4 to 5.
 2. Raise the sum to its 5th power.
then
 3. Multiply the 5th power of the sum by 3.
 4. Add 2 to the product.
 5. Divide the sum by 7.
Hence press

$$\underbrace{[4][+][5]}_{1}\underbrace{[\times][=][=][=][=]}_{2}\underbrace{[\times][3]}_{3}\underbrace{[+][2]}_{4}\underbrace{[\div][7][=]}_{5}$$

RTR: 25307

You will note that we have used the last method mentioned in the chapter concerning the constant as we raised $4 + 5$ to its 5th power. (See p. 8.)

RESTRUCTURING

As mentioned at the beginning of this chapter, it is sometimes necessary to juggle the numbers you have to enter in a computation in order to avoid an overflow of your calculator. This maneuver is possible when two requirements are met. First, the equation has to be in the form of a fraction; second, the quantities in the numerator and in the denominator cannot be separated by addition or subtraction signs. When these requirements are satisfied, one can multiply and divide these numbers (quantities) between them in any order. An example is

$$\frac{52420 \times 420 \times 52300}{4321 \times 530 \times 510}.$$

Learning to Use Your Calculator

If you performed

52420 ⊠ 420 ⊠ 52300 ⊞ 4321 ⊞ 530 ⊞ 510 ⊟

you would reach an overflow. To avoid this, you can restructure the equation:

52420 ⊞ 4321 ⊠ 420 ⊞ 530 ⊠ 52300 ⊞ 510 ⊟

and reach the answer 1006.8364. This is equivalent to computing

$$\frac{52420}{4321} \times \frac{420}{530} \times \frac{52300}{510} = 985.8655$$

Here is another example that should demonstrate the meaning of "quantity." Solve

$$\frac{481(45623002 + 36529642)}{6476255}.$$

Since 45623002 + 36529642 is between parentheses, this sum is considered as one quantity, and thus the requirements stated above are fulfilled. To solve this equation we shall compute it as if it were written as

$$\frac{45623002 + 36529642}{6476255} (481).$$

This avoids an overflow:

45623002 ⊞ 36529642 ⊞ 6476255 ⊠ 481 ⊟ RTR: 6101.585

Here are a few formulas that might help you in using that maneuvering technique:

$\dfrac{A \times B}{C \times D}$ can be solved with

$A \boxtimes B \boxplus C \boxplus D \boxminus$

or $A \boxplus C \boxplus D \boxtimes B \boxminus$

or $A \boxplus C \boxtimes B \boxplus D \boxminus$

or $C \boxtimes D \boxplus \boxminus \boxminus \boxtimes A \boxtimes B \boxminus$

$\dfrac{A + B}{C \times D}$ can be solved with

$A \boxplus B \boxplus C \boxplus D \boxminus$

or $A \boxplus C \boxplus D \boxminus$ (WTR = R) $B \boxplus C \boxplus D \boxplus R \boxminus$

$\dfrac{A \times B}{C + D}$ can be solved with

$C \boxplus D \boxplus \boxminus \boxminus \boxtimes A \boxtimes B \boxminus$

or $C \boxplus D \boxminus$ (WTR = R) $A \boxplus R \boxtimes B \boxminus$

or $C \boxplus D \boxminus$ (WTR = R) $A \boxtimes B \boxplus R \boxminus$

$\dfrac{A + B}{C + D}$ can be solved with

$C \boxplus D \boxminus$ (WTR = R) $A \boxplus B \boxplus R \boxminus$

or $C \boxplus D \boxminus$ (WTR = R) $A \boxplus R \boxminus$ (WTR = S) $B \boxplus R \boxplus S \boxminus$

or $A \boxplus B \boxminus$ (WTR = R) $C \boxplus D \boxplus \boxminus \boxminus \boxtimes R \boxminus$

As mentioned before, the reciprocal of a number can be obtained on most calculators by entering that number, pressing $\boxplus$ once, and then $\boxminus$ twice (see p. 12). The reciprocal can sometimes be very useful in a chain calculation as it can allow the transfer of a division into a multiplication and thus restructure some steps very conveniently.

Normally the solution of an equation like 15/(2 + 3) requires two steps separated by the inscription of an intermediate result.

[1] 2 ⊞ 3 ⊟   WTR: 5
[2] 15 ⊡ 5 ⊟   RTR: 3

It is however possible to solve such equations with:

2 ⊞ 3 ⊡ ⊟ ⊟ ⊠ 15 ⊟   RTR: 3

where we took the reciprocal of (5 + 3) and multiplied it by 15. To solve 150/[(22 + 13)3]:

22 ⊞ 13 ⊠ 3 ⊡ ⊟ ⊟ ⊠ 150 ⊟   RTR: 1.42857

Of especial interest is

$\frac{A}{B} + \frac{C}{D}$ can be solved with

A ⊡ B ⊠ D ⊞ C ⊡ D ⊟

and

$AB + CD$ can be solved with

A ⊠ B ⊡ D ⊞ C ⊠ D ⊟

PART TWO
SOLVING COMMON PROBLEMS

CHAPTER 4

THE RULE OF THREE

A quantity (*A*) can vary directly *or* inversely as another quantity (*B*). Example: The amount of work (*A*) done by a number (*B*) of workers varies directly as this number varies. On the other hand, the time (*A*) necessary for the completion of a job varies inversely as the number (*B*) of workers assigned to it.

In problems where the *rule of three* is applied, three related quantities are known and a fourth one is unknown. The first two known quantities will have the same relation as the third known quantity will have to the unknown quantity (X). This relation is either direct or inverse.

SOLVING THE RULE OF THREE

There are two ways to solve a problem involving the rule of three.

Direct Variation

If 35 lbs. of a product cost $42, what will be the price of 50 lbs. of the same product? This can be solved by the proportion or by

33

the reduction to the unit. Taking these in order, a *proportion* is the equality of two ratios (fractions). For example, 3/4 and 15/20 form the proportion

$$\frac{3}{4} = \frac{15}{20},$$

in which 3 is to 4 as 15 is to 20. The proportion contains 4 terms. The first and the fourth (3 and 20) are the *extremes*; the second and the third (4 and 15) are the *means*.

In all proportions, the product of the extremes is equal to the product of the means. Thus, $3 \times 20 = 4 \times 15$; indeed, $60 = 60$.

In our example 35 lbs. corresponds to $42 and 50 lbs. corresponds to $X. Thus, one can write the proportion

$$\frac{X}{42} = \frac{50}{35}.$$

Now we need a little algebraic manipulation to isolate the unknown X on one side of the equal sign. Multiply both fractions by 42:

$$\frac{42X}{42} = \frac{(50)(42)}{35}$$

Simplify:

$$\frac{\cancel{42}X}{\cancel{42}} = \frac{(50)(42)}{35}$$

We then have:

$$X = \frac{(50)(42)}{35}$$

With the calculator we compute:

5 0 ☒ 4 2 ⊞ 3 5 ⊟ and   RTR: 60

Solving Common Problems

Hence 50 lbs. of the product will cost $60.

The other method of solution is by *the reduction to the unit*. If 35 lbs. cost $42, 1 lb. costs 42/35 and 50 lbs. will cost 50 (42/35). We find the same equation we had when solving "by the proportion."

$$X = \frac{(50)(42)}{35} = \$60$$

50 ⊠ 42 ⊞ 35 ⊟   RTR: 60

Take another problem: A train travels at a speed of 50 miles per hour for 6 hours. What is the distance covered?

Here X miles corresponds to 6 hours and 50 miles corresponds to 1 hour. We write the proportion

$$\frac{X}{50} = \frac{6}{1}.$$

We isolate the unknown to one side of the equal sign and get $X = (50)(6) = 300$ miles. The "reduction to the unit" will yield the same result: Since 50 miles are covered in one hour, $(50)(6)$ miles, or 300 miles, will be covered in 6 hours.

A last example: A car burned 196 gallons of gas during a 3528-mile trip. What is its average consumption per mile?

196 ⊞ 3528 ⊟ 0.0$\underline{5}$ gallon per mile.

If the question is reversed we get: What is the performance of the car in miles per gallon?

3528 ⊞ 196 ⊟ 18 miles per gallon.

You will notice that since the question was reversed, the last answer is the reciprocal of the first:

$$\frac{1}{18} = 0.0\underline{5} \quad \text{and} \quad \frac{1}{0.0\underline{5}} = 18$$

Inverse Variation

A good example here is the following: 4 salespersons worked 20 hours to complete an inventory. How many salespersons should there have been to accomplish this assignment in 8 hours?

Now, how does one know that a variation is inverse instead of direct? This is quite simple, if you apply the following reasoning: If one quantity increases as the other one increases, we have a direct variation. If one quantity decreases as the other one increases, we have an inverse variation. (Of course, if one quantity decreases as the other decreases, we have a direct variation.)

It is a simple matter of judgment to discover the correct method. The more gallons: the more miles is a direct variation. The fewer hours: the more workers is an inverse variation. The fewer hours: the fewer payroll dollars is a direct variation. ("The more the merrier" is also a direct variation.) To return to the inventory example, here again there are two methods to solve the problem. "By the proportion," we write the equation as if it involved a direct variation (which it doesn't).

$$\frac{X \text{ people}}{4 \text{ people}} = \frac{8 \text{ hours}}{20 \text{ hours}}$$

Since this is an inverse variation, we write the proportion with the second ratio *upside down*:

$$\frac{X \text{ people}}{4 \text{ people}} = \frac{20 \text{ hours}}{8 \text{ hours}},$$

and solve as follows:

$$X = \frac{(20)(4)}{8} = 10 \text{ people}$$

20 ⊠ 4 ⊞ 8 ⊟   RTR: 10

Solving Common Problems

In "reduction to the unit," if 4 people worked 20 hours to accomplish a job, one person would have needed (4)(20) hours (four times longer), or 80 hours. If one person needs 80 hours to accomplish a job, the number of people necessary to complete the same task in 8 hours would be 80/8 people, or 10 people. Here again we find the same result through two different mental processes.

CHAPTER 5

PERCENTAGE

The symbol % is read "percent" and means *per hundred*. The symbol ‰ is read and means *per thousand*. A percent can be expressed in two ways: 5% = 0.05 or 5/100; 125% = 1.25; 980‰ = 0.98; 1/4% = 0.0025.

For our purposes, we shall call the first form *percent* and the second (the decimal fraction) *rate*. Hence

$$\frac{\text{PERCENT}}{100} = \text{RATE}$$

and

$$\text{RATE} \times 100 = \text{PERCENT}$$

A percentage is computed on a quantity called the *base*. As you will see later, the choice of the correct base is an important phase in such calculation. *The base is always equal to 100%.* Let's see how we can use our rule of three to arrive at a general formula for solving percentage problems. Example: What is 4% of $800? Since $800 is the quantity on which 4% is computed, $800 will be the base. We start, as in the "reduction to the unit" method, with the following: If 100% is equal to $800, 1% is equal to $800/100 = $8. If 1% is equal to $8, 4% will equal 4 ×$8 = $32.

As an equation we have

$$X = \frac{(800)(4)}{100}.$$

We can transform this equation to get

$$X = \frac{4}{100}(800).$$

Since the base is always equal to 100%, we can replace 4/100 with 0.04, which you can recognize as being the rate.

Now we have $(0.04)(800) = \$32$, where 0.04 is the *rate*, 800 is the *base*, and 32 is the *percentage*. The general formula is thus

$$\text{PERCENTAGE} = \text{RATE} \times \text{BASE}$$

To repeat, be sure to divide the percent figure by 100 (either mentally or with your calculator) to get the rate.

Examples: What is 3/4% of 52? Mentally compute $3/4\% = 0.75/100 = 0.0075 = $ rate, and with your calculator:

$$52 \; \boxed{\times} \; 0.0075 \; \boxed{=} \quad \text{RTR: 0.39}$$

To find 3.5% of 105 compute

$$105 \; \boxed{\times} \; 0.035 \; \boxed{=} \quad \text{RTR: 3.675}$$

To find 110% of 55 compute

$$55 \; \boxed{\times} \; 1.1 \; \boxed{=} \quad \text{RTR: 60.5}$$

To find 20%, 40%, 50%, 60%, 80%, 150% of 12, we can use our calculator's constant:

20%: $12 \; \boxed{\times} \; 0.2 \; \boxed{=} \quad$ RTR: 2.4
(the base 12 is now in the calculator ...)

Solving Common Problems

40%:	0.4 =	RTR: 4.8
50%:	0.5 =	RTR: 6
60%:	0.6 =	RTR: 7.2
80%:	0.8 =	RTR: 9.6
150%:	1.5 =	RTR: 18

Use the following formula to determine what percent one number is of another:

$$\text{RATE} = \frac{\text{PERCENTAGE}}{\text{BASE}}$$

Remember that the rate (or answer to the last formula) is the percent divided by 100 (a decimal fraction). In order to arrive at a percent you will have to multiply that rate by 100. An example is, 80 is what percent of 90? Since we use the word *of* before 90, the base is 90. In other words 90 will equal 100%. We compute

80 ÷ 90 =   RTR: 0.8

The percent is thus 88.8% (since 0.8888888 × 100 = 88.888888). To find out what percent 90 is of 80 we compute

90 ÷ 80 =   RTR: 1.125

The percent is thus 112.5% (here 80 is equal to 100%).

Generalized Steps: Percentage, Rate, Base, and Percent

PERCENT ÷ 100 × BASE = RTR: *Percentage*
or
RATE × BASE = RTR: *Percentage*
PERCENTAGE ÷ BASE = RTR: *Rate*

PERCENTAGE ÷ RATE = RTR: *Base*

PERCENTAGE ÷ BASE × 100 = RTR: *Percent*

PERCENTAGE ÷ PERCENT × 100 = RTR: *Base*

RATE × 100 = RTR: *Percent*

PERCENT ÷ 100 = RTR: *Rate*

To check your computation, remember the following:

If percent > [†]100, then percentage > base.
If percent < [††]100, then percentage < base.
If percent = 100, then percentage = base.

or

If rate > 1, then percentage > base.
If rate < 1, then percentage < base.
If rate = 1, then percentage = base.

Suppose that, in preparing your tax return, you want to know how much of your income was spent on state sales tax. You know that the total amount spent on taxable items was $8640 (tax included) and that the sales tax in your state is 8%. This is a good example of a computation that requires a careful choice of the base (100%).

If you buy an item costing $20, you will pay $20 plus 8% of $20—$20 is thus your base. The final cost (tax included) will be 100% + 8% of $20, or 1.08 × 20 = $21.60 = 108% of 20. In your tax calculation the $8640 will then equal 108%, and you will want to get the 8% (representing the sales tax). Applying the simple rule of three, since $8640 is equal to 108%, 1% is equal to

---

[†] > means "is greater than"
[††] < means "is less than" See p. 10.

Solving Common Problems

8640/108 = 80. If 1% is equal to 80, then 8% is equal to 8 × 80, or $640.

$$8640 \;\boxed{\div}\; 108 \;\boxed{\times}\; 8 \;\boxed{=} \qquad \text{RTR: 640}$$

Verification:

108%	$8640	Cost (tax included)
− 8%	−$ 640	Tax (8%)
100%	$8000	Selling price

Indeed, $640 is equal to 8% of $8000.

THE MARKUP

We will define the *margin* as the difference between the selling price and the buying price of an item. The *markup* is a percent (of which the margin is the percentage). Remember to enter the markup as a rate (decimal fraction) in the following formulas.

There are two kinds of markup: (1) markup on cost; (2) markup on selling price. When we use the markup on cost, the base (100%) is the buying price. When we use the markup on selling price, it is this last quantity that becomes the base. We define them as follows:

		Example
Buying price	= B	= $ ($140)
Selling price	= S	= $ ($175)
Margin (percentage)	= D	= $ ($ 35)
Markup on cost	= Mb	= % (25% = 0.25)
Markup on selling price	= Ms	= % (20% = 0.20)

Again, remember to enter Mb and Ms as a rate (the percent figure divided by 100).

Generalized Steps

Here are all the formulas (numbered) you could need in solving such problems:

BUYING PRICE (UNKNOWN) (KNOWN)

[1] $\qquad B = S - D \qquad$ S D

$S \boxed{-} D \boxed{=}$

[2] $\qquad B = \dfrac{S}{1 + Mb} \qquad$ S Mb

$1 \boxed{+} Mb \boxed{\div} \boxed{=} \boxed{=} \boxed{\times} S \boxed{=}$

[3] $\qquad B = \dfrac{D}{Mb} \qquad$ D Mb

$D \boxed{\div} Mb \boxed{=}$

[4] $\qquad B = S(1 - Ms) \qquad$ S Ms

$1 \boxed{-} Ms \boxed{\times} S \boxed{=}$

[5] $\qquad B = \dfrac{D(1 - Ms)}{Ms} \qquad$ D Ms

$1 \boxed{-} Ms \boxed{\times} D \boxed{\div} Ms \boxed{=}$

SELLING PRICE (UNKNOWN) (KNOWN)

[6] $\qquad S = B + D \qquad$ B D

$B \boxed{+} D \boxed{=}$

[7] $\qquad S = \dfrac{D}{Ms} \qquad$ D Ms

$D \boxed{\div} Ms \boxed{=}$

Solving Common Problems 45

[8] $$S = \frac{D(1 + Mb)}{Mb}$$ D   Mb

1 $\boxplus$ Mb $\boxtimes$ D $\boxplus$ Mb $\boxminus$

[9] $$S = B(1 + Mb)$$ B   Mb

1 $\boxplus$ Mb $\boxtimes$ B $\boxminus$

[10] $$S = \frac{B}{1 - Ms}$$ B   Ms

1 $\boxminus$ Ms $\boxplus$ $\boxminus$ $\boxminus$ $\boxtimes$ B $\boxminus$

MARGIN (UNKNOWN)   (KNOWN)

[11] $D = S - B$ S   B

S $\boxminus$ B $\boxminus$

[12] $$D = \frac{Mb \cdot S}{Mb + 1}$$ S   Mb

Mb $\boxplus$ 1 $\boxplus$ $\boxminus$ $\boxminus$ $\boxtimes$ Mb $\boxtimes$ S $\boxminus$

[13] $D = Ms \cdot S$ S   Ms

Ms $\boxtimes$ S $\boxminus$

[14] $D = Mb \cdot B$ B   Mb

Mb $\boxtimes$ B $\boxminus$

[15] $$D = \frac{B \cdot Ms}{1 - Ms}$$ B   Ms

1 $\boxminus$ Ms $\boxplus$ $\boxminus$ $\boxminus$ $\boxtimes$ B $\boxtimes$ Ms $\boxminus$

MARKUP ON COST (UNKNOWN) (KNOWN)

[16] $$Mb = \frac{Ms}{1 - Ms}$$ Ms

1 ⊟ Ms ⊞ ⊟ ⊟ ⊠ Ms ⊟

[17] $$Mb = \frac{S - B}{B}$$ S B

S ⊟ B ⊞ B ⊟

[18] $$Mb = \frac{D}{B}$$ B D

D ⊞ B ⊟

[19] $$Mb = \frac{D}{S - D}$$ S D

S ⊟ D ⊞ ⊟ ⊟ ⊠ D ⊟

MARKUP ON SELLING PRICE (UNKNOWN) (KNOWN)

[20] $$Ms = \frac{D}{B + D}$$ B D

B ⊞ D ⊞ ⊟ ⊟ ⊠ D ⊟

[21] $$Ms = \frac{D}{S}$$ S D

D ⊞ S ⊟

[22] $$Ms = \frac{Mb}{Mb + 1}$$ Mb

1 ⊞ Mb ⊞ ⊟ ⊟ ⊠ Mb ⊟

[23] $$Ms = \frac{S - B}{S}$$ S B

S ⊟ B ⊞ S ⊟

Solving Common Problems

Obviously, the results to these last eight formulas will be rates. Remember to multiply them by 100 to get the percent figure.

Example: A merchant purchases a table for $105 and wants a markup of 60% above his cost. At what price will the table be sold and what will the margin be?

(Formula #9) $S = B(Mb + 1) = 105(0.6 + 1)$

Compute: 0.6 ⊞ 1 ⊠ 105 ⊟   RTR: $168

The margin will then be $168 − $105 = $63, and indeed $63 is 60% of $105.

Example: The same merchant wants a markup on the selling price of 37.5% (same buying price of $105).

(Formula #10) $S = \dfrac{B}{1 - Ms} = \dfrac{105}{1 - 0.375}$

1 ⊟ 0.375 ⊞ ⊟ ⊟ ⊠ 105 ⊟   RTR: $168

The selling price here is identical to the result in the first example: $168 − $105 = a margin of $63, which is indeed equivalent to 37.5% of $168. Let's check that a markup on cost of 60% corresponds to a markup on the selling price of 37.5%.

(Formula #22) $Ms = \dfrac{Mb}{Mb + 1} = \dfrac{0.6}{0.6 + 1}$

0.6 ⊞ 1 ⊞ ⊟ ⊟ ⊠ 0.6 ⊟ RTR: 0.375

You notice that to compute a markup on cost *from* a markup on the selling price (or vice versa) no other *given* is necessary. Indeed, the buying price, selling price, or margin do not affect that calculation. No matter how much an item costs, if a markup (%) is chosen, the "other" markup will always stay the same as the result of formulas 22 or 16, depending on the known type of markup.

Consider formula #9 again for tackling the discount problems. With this formula, $S = B(Mb + 1)$, we find the selling price of an item knowing its cost and its markup (on cost). Let's see how we arrive at this formula.

If an item costs $100 and its markup is 60%, the margin will be $0.6 \times 100 = \$60$. The selling price is thus $\$100 + \$60 = \$160$.

We can arrive at the same result more quickly by adding the markup % to the base % (always 100%) and then finally finding the percentage (which will in that case be the selling price). Thus, adding 60% to 100% yields 160%, which is indeed the selling price of the item: $1.6 \times 100 = \$160$. The same reasoning applies to any buying price and markup (on cost).

Example: Find the selling price of an item costing $54.50 with a markup on cost of 65%. Since 100% + 65% = 165%, the selling price will be 165% of the buying price. We then have $1.65 \times 54.5 = \$89.93$.

DISCOUNT

Discount is the diminution or reduction of a price (markdown). As we added the markup to 100% to find a higher figure as selling price, here we *subtract* the discount from 100% (the base) and simply multiply the original price by this new percent to find the reduced price. For example, if a discount of 15% is applied on an item costing $120, what is the new reduced price? First, 100% − 15% = 85%, so that the new price is then 85% of $120. Hence $0.85 \times 120 = 102$. And indeed, this difference ($120 − 102 = \$18$) is equal to 15% of $120: $0.15 \times 120 = 18$. This method is represented by the formula

REDUCED PRICE = ORIGINAL PRICE (1 − DISCOUNT RATE)

Example: If the original price is $85 and the discount is 20%, the discount rate is 0.2. We then have $\$85(1 − 0.2) = \$85 \times 0.8 = \$68$.

Solving Common Problems 49

Example: If the original price is $132 and the discount is 33⅓%, the discount rate is 0.3̄. Then $132(1 − 0.3̄) = $132 × 0.6̄ = $88.

If you understand that a discount is a *negative markup*, you will be able to use all the formulas given for the markup (on cost or on the selling price) by simply entering Mb or Ms as a negative figure.

MULTIPLE TRADE DISCOUNTS

A variation of the discount principle is the multiple trade discounts, otherwise known as the successive trade discounts. A company may offer two trade discounts, 20% and 5%. One customer may be entitled to a 20% discount and another will get 5%, depending on status (jobber, wholesaler, retailer, etc.), and a third customer of a different status will receive 20% *and* 5%. For this third customer, the price of an item originally sold at $82 is $62.32. The two discounts *cannot* be simply added together (20% + 5% = 25% is inapplicable). You have to use the following formula:

EQUIVALENT TRADE DISCOUNT *RATE* = E

E = (FIRST *RATE* + SECOND *RATE*) − (FIRST *RATE* × SECOND *RATE*)

and

REDUCED PRICE = ORIGINAL PRICE (1 − E)

Example: If the original price is $135 and the trade discounts are 20% and 15%, we have 135{1 − [(0.2 + 0.15) − (0.2 × 0.15)]}, which is equal to $91.80. Doing this the long way: 20% of $135 is $27; $135 − $27 = $108; 15% of $108 is $16.20; $108 − $16.20 = $91.80.

Example: If the original price is $208.50 and the trade

discounts are 15% and 12½%, we have 208.5{1 − [(0.15 + 0.125) − (0.15 × 0.125)]}. With your calculator you need only *one* chain calculation to solve this equation! If we remove the aggregation symbols, we get:

0.15 ⊠ 0.125 ⊞ 1 ⊟ 0.15 ⊟ 0.125 ⊠ 208.5 ⊟   RTR: $155.07

Generalized Steps: Multiple Trade Discounts

FIRST RATE ⊠ SECOND RATE ⊞ 1 ⊟
FIRST RATE ⊟ SECOND RATE
⊠ ORIGINAL PRICE ⊟ NEW REDUCED PRICE

Remember again that a rate is the percent *divided by 100*.

Example: If the original price is $637.23 and the discounts are 23% and 17%:

0.23 ⊠ 0.17 ⊞ 1 ⊟ 0.23 ⊟ 0.17 ⊠ 637.23 ⊟
RTR: 407.25

CHAPTER 6

CONVERSIONS

This chapter contains one formula for each type of conversion and an example of its use. In these examples the abbreviations (or symbols) of each type of quantity will be used and the answers will show two decimals.

LENGTH

The factors here are *exact and not approximations* (unless otherwise noted, miles refers to the statute mile).

U.S. to Metric

Miles × 1.609344 = Kilometers
    3 mi. ⊠ 1.609344 ▣ 4.83 km.
Miles × 1609.344 = Meters
    5 mi. ⊠ 1609.344 ▣ 8046.72 m.
Miles (naut.) × 1.852 = Kilometers
    3 naut. mi. ⊠ 1.852 ▣ 5.56 km.
Yards × 0.9144 = Meters
    3 yd. ⊠ 0.9144 ▣ 2.74 m.

Feet × 0.3048 = Meters
    12 ft. ☒ 0.3048 ☐ 3.66 m.
Feet × 30.48 = Centimeters
    2 ft. ☒ 30.48 ☐ 60.96 cm.
Inches × 2.54 = Centimeters
    15 in. ☒ 2.54 ☐ 38.10 cm.
Inches × 25.4 = Millimeters
    3 in. ☒ 25.4 ☐ 76.20 mm.

Metric to U.S.

Kilometers ÷ 1.609344 = Miles
    5 km ÷ 1.609344 ☐ 3.11 mi
Meters ÷ 1609.344 = Miles
    560 m ÷ 1609.344 ☐ 0.35 mi
Meters ÷ 0.9144 = Yards
    3 m ÷ 0.9144 ☐ 3.28 yd
Meters ÷ 0.3048 = Feet
    5 m ÷ 0.3048 ☐ 16.40 ft
Centimeters ÷ 30.48 = Feet
    58 cm ÷ 30.48 ☐ 1.90 ft
Centimeters ÷ 2.54 = Inches
    52 cm ÷ 2.54 ☐ 20.47 in
Millimeters ÷ 25.4 = Inches
    48 mm ÷ 25.4 ☐ 1.89 in

U.S. to U.S.

Miles × 5280 = Feet
    3 mi ☒ 5280 ☐ 15840 ft
Miles × 1760 = Yards
    4 mi ☒ 1760 ☐ 7040 yd
Yards × 3 = Feet
    9 yd ☒ 3 ☐ 27 ft
Yards × 36 = Inches
    4 yd ☒ 36 ☐ 144 in

Solving Common Problems 53

Feet × 12 = Inches
$\qquad$ 5 ft ⊠ 12 ⊟ 60 in

Metric to Metric

Kilometers × 1000 = Meters
$\qquad$ 3 km ⊠ 1000 ⊟ 3000 m
Meters × 100 = Centimeters
$\qquad$ 5 m ⊠ 100 ⊟ 500 cm
Centimeters × 10 = Millimeters
$\qquad$ 15 cm ⊠ 10 ⊟ 150 mm

AREA

Here the factors have a maximum of 10 significant digits or are exact to one part in a billion!

U.S. to Metric

Acres × 4046.856422 = Square Meters
$\qquad$ 3 a ⊠ 4046.856422 ⊟ 12140.57 m^2
Acres × 0.4046856422 = Hectares
$\qquad$ 11 a ⊠ 0.4046856422 ⊟ 4.45 h
Square Miles × 2.589988110 = Square Kilometers
$\qquad$ 36 sq mi ⊠ 2.58998811 ⊟ 93.24 km^2
Square Miles × 2589988.110 = Square Meters
$\qquad$ 36 sq mi ⊠ 2589988.11 ⊟ 93239571.96 m^2
Square Yards × 0.83612736 = Square Meters
$\qquad$ 11 sq yd ⊠ 0.83612736 ⊟ 9.20 m^2
Square Feet × 0.09290304 = Square Meters
$\qquad$ 25 sq ft ⊠ 0.09290304 ⊟ 2.32 m^2
Square Feet × 929.0304 = Square Centimeters
$\qquad$ 5 sq ft ⊠ 929.0304 ⊟ 4645.15 cm^2
Square Inches × 6.4516 = Square Centimeters
$\qquad$ 31 sq in ⊠ 6.4516 ⊟ 200 cm^2

Square Inches × 645.16 = Square Millimeters
21 sq in ☒ 645.16 ☐ 13548.36 mm²

Metric to U.S.

As you may have already gathered, one can use the same factors stated above: Simply divide the metric quantity by the related factor to get the corresponding quantity in U.S. measure. For example, to convert 11 hectares to acres, Compute:

11 ☐ 0.4046856422 ☐   RTR: 27.18 a

U.S. to U.S.

Square Miles × 640 = Acres
2 sq mi ☒ 640 ☐ 1280 a
Square Miles × 27878400 = Square Feet
0.5 sq mi ☒ 27878400 ☐ 13939200 sq ft
Square Yards × 9 = Square Feet
6 sq yd ☒ 9 ☐ 54 sq ft
Square Yards × 1296 = Square Inches
21 sq yd ☒ 1296 ☐ 27216 sq in
Square Feet × 144 = Square Inches
5 sq ft ☒ 144 ☐ 720 sq in

Metric to Metric

Hectares × 10000 = Square Meters
2 h ☒ 10000 ☐ 20000 m²
Square Kilometers × 1000000 = Square Meters
0.2 km² ☒ 1000000 ☐ 200000 m²
Square Meters × 10000 = Square Centimeters
1.5 m² ☒ 10000 ☐ 15000 cm²

Solving Common Problems

VOLUME (and liquid measures)

U.S. to Metric

Cubic Feet × 0.028316847 = Cubic Meters
 9 cu ft ⊠ 0.028316847 ▣ 0.25 m³
Cubic Inches × 16.387064 = Cubic Centimeters
 5 cu in ⊠ 16.387064 ▣ 81.94 cm³
Gallons × 3.785411784 = Liters
 2 gal ⊠ 3.785411784 ▣ 7.57 l.
Quarts × 0.946352946 = Liters
 2 qt ⊠ 0.946352946 ▣ 1.89 l.
Pints × 0.473176473 = Liters
 3 pt ⊠ 0.473176473 ▣ 1.42 l.

Metric to U.S.

(Same remark as for area conversions.)

U.S. to U.S.

Cubic Feet × 1728 = Cubic Inches
 0.5 cu ft ⊠ 1728 ▣ 864 cu in
Gallons × 231 = Cubic Inches
 2 gal ⊠ 231 ▣ 462 cu in
Quarts × 57.75 = Cubic Inches
 4 qt ⊠ 57.75 ▣ 231 cu in
Pints ⊠ 28.875 = Cubic Inches
 8 pt ⊠ 28.875 ▣ 231 cu in

Metric to Metric

Cubic Meters × 1000 = Liters
　　　　　0.5 m³ ☒ 1000 ☐ 500 l.
Cubic Decimeters × 1 = Liters
　　　　　5 dm³ ☒ 1 ☐ 5 l.

MASS

U.S. to Metric

Short Tons × 0.90718474 = Tons
　　　　　0.5 tons ☒ 0.90718474 ☐ 0.45 t
Pounds × 0.45359237 = Kilograms
　　　　　138 lbs ☒ 0.45359237 ☐ 62.60 kg
Ounces × 28.349523 = Grams
　　　　　5 oz ☒ 28.349523 ☐ 141.75 g
Troy Ounces × 31.103486 = Grams
　　　　　50 oz t ☒ 31.103486 ☐ 1555.17 g

Metric to U.S.

(Same remark as for area conversions.)

U.S. to U.S.

Short Tons × 2000 = Pounds
　　　　　0.5 tons ☒ 2000 ☐ 1000 lbs
Hundredweights × 100 = Pounds
　　　　　4 cwt ☒ 100 ☐ 400 lbs
Pounds × 16 = Ounces
　　　　　4 lbs ☒ 16 ☐ 64 oz

Solving Common Problems

Metric to Metric

Tons × 1000 = Kilograms
  0.5 t ☒ 1000 ☐ 500 kg
Kilograms × 1000 = Grams
  0.3 kg ☒ 1000 ☐ 300 g

TEMPERATURE

Fahrenheit to Centigrade

$$\frac{5(°F - 32)}{9} = °C$$
212 °F ☐ ③ ② ☒ ⑤ ÷ ⑨ ☐   RTR: 100 °C

Centigrade to Fahrenheit

$$\frac{9 °C}{5} + 32 = °F$$
37 °C ☒ ⑨ ÷ ⑤ ☐ ③ ② ☐   RTR: 98.60 °F

PART THREE
BANKING PROBLEMS

CHAPTER 7

SIMPLE INTEREST

Interest is the money one party pays for the use of another's money. This is a sum of money paid at the end of the period during which the money (the *principal*) has been used. Three elements are necessary for the computation of the interest: (1) the interest rate; (2) the amount of money borrowed or placed (the principal); and (3) the time during which the principal has been borrowed or placed. For our purposes we shall use the following abbreviations:

P (stands for present value) = principal
F (stands for future value) = principal + interest
i = interest rate
n = number of years and/or fraction thereof
I = Interest

The rate of interest is the ratio of the amount of the interest paid (for a given period of time) to the principal (it is usually expressed as a percent and used in computation as a rate: percent/100). If the principal (P = $1000) is borrowed for one year and the interest (I = $70) is simple, then the rate of interest is 70/1000 = 0.07 = 7%.

Remember that i (interest rate) can be expressed in two ways: if i = 7%, then i = 0.07; if i = 12%, then i = 0.12; if i =

0.5%, then $i = 0.005$; and so on. The rate of interest expressed in % is the amount of dollars paid when $100 are borrowed/placed for one year.

The interest varies directly as the time during which the principal has been borrowed or placed. The formula for the simple interest is:

$$I = Pni$$

where n = number of years.

Example: What is the interest paid if $P = \$12000$, $i = 7\%$, and $n = 3$ years?

12000 ⊠ 0.07 ⊠ 3 ⊟   RTR: $2520

The formula for the *future value* (principal + interest) is

$$F = P + I$$

Thus, the future value of the $12000 placed at 7% during 3 years is:

12000 ⊞ 2520 ⊟   RTR: $14520

We can use the more direct method:

$$F = P(1 + ni)$$

to arrive at the same result:

3 ⊠ 0.07 ⊞ 1 ⊠ 12000 ⊟   RTR: $14520

Before giving the various formulas for simple-interest calculations, it is necessary to add a little refinement that will allow us the computation of interest on principal placed/borrowed during a fraction of a year.

Example: What is the interest of a capital $P = \$500$ placed for 90 days at 6%? Since 90 days make up less than a year, we

Banking Problems

have to transform 90 to a fraction of one year: 90/360 = 0.25 (or a quarter of one year).

You will notice that we used 360 as denominator in our equation. Indeed, the usual practice in banking calculation makes use of the "commercial year" or "business year" of 360 days per year and 30 days per month, as opposed to the "civil year" or "calendar year" of 365/6 days. In our example, we then have

$I = Pni$ = 500 ⊠ 0.25 ⊠ 0.06 ⊟   RTR: $7.50
$F = P(1 + ni)$ = 0.25 ⊠ 0.06 ⊞ 1 ⊠ 500 ⊟   RTR: $507.50
Verification: $500 + $7.50 = $507.50

Example: If a capital P = $1300 is borrowed for 450 days at 11%, what will the interest paid be? Again, since the number of days is not equivalent to an integral number of years, we have to transform 450 days to a fraction of year(s): 450/360 = 1.25 (one year plus a quarter of one year). The interest will thus be:

$I = Pni$ = 1300 ⊠ 1.25 ⊠ 0.11 ⊟   RTR: $178.75

What if we want to know the rate of interest that produced an interest of $250 when a principal P = $1600 was placed for one year and a half? Here the formula is:

$$i = \frac{I}{Pn}$$

If n here equals 1.5, we compute:

250 ⊞ 1600 ⊞ 1.5 ⊟   RTR: 0.1041<u>6</u>

The rate expressed in % was then

0.1041<u>6</u> ⊠ 100 ⊟   RTR: 10.42%

If we know the future value, the interest, and the time, we use the following formula to find the interest rate:

$$i = \frac{I}{n(F - I)}$$

Example: A capital sum placed for 50 months (1500 days) yielded $12725, of which $3112 was the interest. What was the rate of interest? We get n with:

50 ÷ 12 = 4.1<u>6</u> or 1500 ÷ 360 = 4.1<u>6</u>

We compute:

12725 − 3112 × 4.1<u>6</u> ÷ = = × 3112 =   RTR: 0.07748

Expressed in % we have:

0.0774<u>8</u> × 100 =   RTR: 7.75%

Here are the generalized steps for simple interest problems:

P = Present value of principal
F = Future value of principal
i = Rate of interest (expressed as a decimal fraction)
I = Interest
n = Number of years (or fraction thereof)

INTEREST (UNKNOWN)   (KNOWN)

[1] $I = F - P$ F P
           F − P =

[2] $I = Pni$ P n i
           P × n × i =

[3] $I = \dfrac{Fni}{1 + ni}$ F n i

n × i + 1 ÷ = = × F × n × i =

Banking Problems

FUTURE VALUE (UNKNOWN)   (KNOWN)

[4] $$F = P + I$$
$P \boxplus I \boxminus$
   $P \quad I$

[5] $$F = P(1 + ni)$$
$n \boxtimes i \boxplus 1 \boxtimes P \boxminus$
   $P \quad n \quad i$

[6] $$F = I + \frac{I}{ni}$$
$I \boxdiv n \boxdiv i \boxplus I \boxminus$
   $I \quad n \quad i$

PRESENT VALUE (UNKNOWN)   (KNOWN)

[7] $$P = F - I$$
$F \boxminus I \boxminus$
   $F \quad I$

[8] $$P = \frac{I}{ni}$$
$I \boxdiv n \boxdiv i \boxminus$
   $I \quad n \quad i$

[9] $$P = \frac{F}{1 + ni}$$
$n \boxtimes i \boxplus 1 \boxdiv \boxminus \boxminus \boxtimes F \boxminus$
   $F \quad n \quad i$

RATE OF INTEREST (UNKNOWN)   (KNOWN)

[10] $$i = \frac{I}{Pn}$$
$I \boxdiv P \boxdiv n \boxminus$
   $I \quad P \quad n$

[11] $$i = \frac{I}{n(F - I)}$$
$F \boxminus I \boxtimes n \boxdiv \boxminus \boxminus \boxtimes I \boxminus$
   $I \quad F \quad n$

[12] $$i = \frac{F - P}{PN}$$ F   P   n

$F \boxminus P \boxplus P \boxplus n \boxminus$

TIME (UNKNOWN)   (KNOWN)

[13] $$n = \frac{I}{Pi}$$ I   P   i

$I \boxplus P \boxplus i \boxminus$

[14] $$n = \frac{I}{i(F - I)}$$ I   F   i

$F \boxminus I \boxtimes i \boxplus \boxminus \boxminus \boxtimes I \boxminus$

[15] $$n = \frac{F - P}{Pi}$$ F   P   i

$F \boxminus P \boxplus P \boxplus i \boxminus$

Note: Always remember that *i* is the *rate* of interest—that is, the figure in % divided by 100.

CHAPTER 8

COMPOUND INTEREST

Compound interest is the amount of money paid at the end of each period on the principal *and on the accumulated interest*. For example, if $2000 is placed during two years at 5% (compounded annually), at the end of the first year the interest will be:

$2000 ⊠ 0.05 (⊠ 1) ⊟   RTR: $100

The future value at the end of the first year is then $2000 + $100 = $2100. Now the interest for the second year will be computed on $2100, not on $2000. Thus:

$2100 ⊠ 0.05 (⊠ 1) ⊟   RTR: 105

The future value at the end of the placement (2 years) will be $2100 + $105 = $2205.

If the $2000 had been placed at simple interest, the future value would have been:

2 ⊠ 0.05 ⊞ 1 ⊠ 2000 ⊟   RTR: $2200

There is a difference of $5 between the two results. This difference becomes greater as the time during which the principal is placed is longer.

Compound interest can be compounded annually (at the end of each year), semiannually (at the end of each semester), quarterly (at the end of each quarter), monthly, or sometimes even daily. If no special period is mentioned, it is usually understood that the interest is compounded annually.

Let's first become familiar with the formula for the computation of the future value of the principal (or accumulated amount after n years) placed at a rate of interest compounded annually.

$$F = P(1+i)^n$$

where P = Present value (principal)
F = Future value (accumulated amount)
i = Interest rate (decimal fraction)
n = Number of years (an integer)

Example: If the principal (P = $12500) is deposited for 5 years at a known rate (i = 4%, compounded annually), then F = $12500(1 + 0.04)^5$ = $15208.16. (The generalized steps will be shown later.) Obviously the interest is then $15208.16 − $12500 = $2708.16.

If the interest in this example had been compounded semiannually, we would have used the following formula:

$$F = P\left(1 + \frac{i}{q}\right)^{nq}$$

where q is the number of times the interest is compounded during one year. When the interest is compounded twice each year (semianually)—hence, $q = 2$—we have:

$$F = 12500\left(1 + \frac{0.04}{2}\right)^{5 \cdot 2} =$$

$$F = 12500(1 + 0.02)^{10} = \$15237.43$$

Example: A principal (P = $8000) is placed for 6 years at 5 ¼% compounded quarterly. What will the future value be? The calculations are:

Banking Problems

$$F = 8000\left(1 + \frac{0.0525}{4}\right)^{6 \cdot 4} = \$10939.62$$

1. Number of times the interest is compounded in one year ⊠ number of years ⊟
2. WTR = N
3. Rate (in decimal) ⊞ number of times the interest is compounded in one year ⊞ 1 ⊠ ⊟ ... (Press ⊟ N minus one times) ⊠ principal ⊟ *Future Value*

Here again we use the constant on our calculator as shown in the generalzed steps for the compounded interest problems. The number of years has to be an integer. If n isn't an integer, we shall use the generalized steps given on p. 71.

Consider our previous example, $P = \$8000$; $N = 6$; $i = 5\frac{1}{4}\%$; $q = 4$.

1. 4 ⊠ 6 ⊟   WTR: 24
2. $N = 24$
3. 0.0525 ⊞ 4 ⊞ 1 ⊠ ⊟ ⊠ 8000 ⊟
   RTR: $10939.62   (We pressed ⊟ 23 times in step (3), since $N = 24$)

Example: $P = \$250000$ at $4\frac{3}{4}\%$ semiannually for 2 years. What is F?

1. 2 ⊠ 2 ⊟   WTR: 4
2. $N = 4$
3. 0.0475 ⊞ 2 ⊞ 1 ⊠ ⊟ ⊟ ⊟ ⊠ 250000 ⊟
   RTR: $274609.52

If you need to compute the future value of principal that is placed for a period of time that cannot be expressed as an integer, you will need a mixed method, whereby you first get the future value with the compound interest formula for a period that can be divided into a maximum number of years (as an integer) and then complete your calculation with the simple interest formula.

Example: What will be the future value of a principal of $2500 placed for 860 days at 5%, compounded quarterly? We first decompose our 860 days into years, quarters, and remaining days (if any):

$$860 \boxed{\div} 360 \boxed{=} \text{ RTR: } 2.3\underline{8} \text{ (two years and } 0.3\underline{8})$$
$$0.3\underline{8} \boxed{\times} 4 \boxed{=} \text{ RTR: } 1.\underline{5} \text{ (one quarter and } 0.\underline{5})$$
$$0.\underline{5} \boxed{\times} 90 \boxed{=} \text{ RTR: } 50 \text{ (50 days)}$$

Checking the calculations, 720 days (two years = 2 × 360) plus 90 days (one quarter = 1 × 90) plus 50 days equals 860 days. The future value after two years will be:

$$0.05 \boxed{\div} 4 \boxed{+} 1 \boxed{\times} \boxed{=} \boxed{=} \boxed{=} \boxed{=} \boxed{=} \boxed{=} \boxed{=} \boxed{\times} 2500 \boxed{=}$$
WTR: 2761.2145

The future value after two years and one quarter will be:

$$0.05 \boxed{\times} 90 \boxed{\div} 360 \boxed{+} 1 \boxed{\times} 2761.2145 \boxed{=}$$
WTR: 2795.7296

The future value after the 860 days will be:

$$0.05 \boxed{\times} 50 \boxed{\div} 360 \boxed{+} 1 \boxed{\times} 2795.7296 \boxed{=}$$
RTR: $2815.14

The equations for these problems are, respectively

$$2500 \left(1 + \frac{0.05}{4}\right)^{2 \cdot 4} = 2761.2145$$

$$2761.2145 \left(1 + \frac{0.05 \cdot 90}{360}\right) = 2795.7296$$

$$2795.7296 \left(1 + \frac{0.05 \cdot 50}{360}\right) = 2815.1442$$

Banking Problems

And here is a formula that you can use in all cases:

$$F = \frac{P\left\{\left[i\left(N - \frac{360 \cdot Y}{q}\right)\right] + 360\right\}\left(1 + \frac{i}{q}\right)^Y}{360}$$

where F = Future value
 P = Present value of principal
 N = Total number of days
 q = Number of times the interest is compounded per year
 i = Rate of interest in decimal fraction (you must enter 5% as 0.05)
 Y = The integral part of $[N \cdot q/360]$—if $N \cdot q/360$ = 3.5\underline{9}, the integral part is 3. The integer is the figure(s) to the left of the decimal point.

Generalized Steps: Compound Interest, Future Value

These allow the introduction of *any* time frame.

1. TOTAL NUMBER OF DAYS ⊠ NUMBER OF TIMES THE INTEREST IS COMPOUNDED PER YEAR ⊞ 360 ⊟
2. Write all the figures on the left of the decimal point WTR (integer) = Y
3. 360 ⊠ Y ⊞ NUMBER OF TIMES THE INTEREST IS COMPOUNDED PER YEAR ⊠ ⊟ 1 ⊞ TOTAL NUMBER OF DAYS ⊠ RATE (remember to enter the decimal fraction) ⊞ 360 ⊟
4. WTR = A
5. RATE OF INTEREST (ditto: in decimal fraction) ⊞ NUMBER OF TIMES THE INTEREST IS COMPOUNDED PER YEAR ⊞ 1 ⊠ ⊟ ... (Press ⊟ Y minus one times) ⊠ A ⊞ 360 ⊠ PRINCIPAL (Present Value) ⊟ *Future Value*

Example: P = 33836.80, i = 5¾% (semiannually); N = 1314 days
1. 1314 ⊠ 2 ⊞ 360 ⊟

2. $Y = 7$
3. 360 $\times$ 7 $\div$ 2 $\times$ $-$ 1 $+$ 1314 $\times$ 0.0575 $+$ 360 $=$
4. $A = 363.105$
5. 0.0575 $\div$ 2 $+$ 1 $\times$ $=$ $=$ $=$ $=$ $=$ $=$ (since $Y = 7$ we press $=$ 6 times) $\times$ 363.105 $\div$ 360 $\times$ 33836.8 $=$
RTR: $41618.63

Example: $P = 2500$; $i = 5\%$ (quarterly); $N = 860$ days.
1. 860 $\times$ 4 $\div$ 360 $=$
2. $Y = 9$
3. 360 $\times$ 9 $\div$ 4 $\times$ $-$ 1 $+$ 860 $\times$ 0.05 $+$ 360 $=$
4. $A = 362.5$
5. 0.05 $\div$ 4 $+$ 1 $\times$ $=$ $=$ $=$ $=$ $=$ $=$ $=$ $=$ $\times$ 362.5 $\div$ 360 $\times$ 2500 $=$
RTR: $2815.14 (which is the same result found with the example given before the generalized steps).

CHAPTER 9

DISCOUNT TO YIELD

As we have just seen in the previous chapter, it is possible to place a known principal at a known rate of interest and expect to retrieve, after a determined period of time, a future value that can be computed.

It also happens (especially when you want to buy a "commercial paper") that you can place a principal (to be computed) at a known rate of interest and expect, after a certain time, to retrieve a known future value. In this instance the rate of interest is called a *discount to yield*.

First instance:
KNOWN PRINCIPAL......... WILL YIELD ....
$10000
 .... UNKNOWN FUTURE VALUE
 $?

Second instance:
UNKNOWN PRINCIPAL........WILL YIELD ....
$?
 .... KNOWN FUTURE VALUE
 $10000

Here is the formula with which you can compute the present

73

value of a principal, knowing the future value, the discount to yield, and the time after which the future value will be retrieved.

$$P = \frac{360 \cdot F}{\left[i \left(N - \frac{360 \cdot Y}{q} \right) + 360 \right] \left(1 + \frac{i}{q} \right)^Y}$$

Where P = Present value of principal
  F = Future value of principal
  i = Discount to yield (as a decimal fraction!)
  N = Total number of days
  q = Number of times the discount to yield is compounded per year
  Y = The integral part of $[N \cdot q/360]$. The integral part is the figure(s) to the left of the decimal point.

Example: How much do you have to invest at a rate (discount to yield) of 4%, if you want to retrieve, in 864 days, a future value of $20000? The rate is compounded annually.

First, let's get Y: $(864 \times 1)/360 = 2.4$; hence $Y = 2$, then

$$P = \frac{360 \cdot 20000}{\left[0.04 \left(864 - \frac{360 \cdot 2}{1} \right) + 360 \right] \left(1 + \frac{0.04}{1} \right)^2}$$

The answer is $18199.44. Let's check it with the following *generalized steps* for the computation of the future value by means of the discount to yield.

Generalized Steps: Discount to Yield, Present Value

1. TOTAL NUMBER OF DAYS ⊠ NUMBER OF TIMES THE DISCOUNT TO YIELD IS COMPOUNDED PER YEAR ⊞ 360 ⊟
2. WTR (integer) = Y
3. 360 ⊠ Y ⊞ NUMBER OF TIMES THE DISCOUNT TO YIELD IS COMPOUNDED PER YEAR ⊠ ⊟ 1 ⊞ TOTAL NUMBER OF DAYS ⊠

Banking Problems 75

    DISCOUNT TO YIELD (decimal fraction) $\boxed{+}$ 360 $\boxed{=}$
4. WTR = *A*
5. DISCOUNT TO YIELD $\boxed{\div}$ NUMBER OF TIMES THE DISCOUNT TO YIELD IS COMPOUNDED PER YEAR $\boxed{+}$ 1 $\boxed{\times}$ $\boxed{=}$ ... (Press $\boxed{=}$ *Y* minus one times) $\boxed{\times}$ *A* $\boxed{\div}$ $\boxed{=}$ $\boxed{=}$ $\boxed{\times}$ 360 $\boxed{\times}$ FUTURE VALUE $\boxed{=}$ *Present Value*

Let's check the previous example on your calculator.
1. 864 $\boxed{\times}$ 1 $\boxed{+}$ 360 $\boxed{=}$
2. *Y* = 2
3. 360 $\boxed{\times}$ 2 $\boxed{\div}$ 1 $\boxed{\times}$ $\boxed{-}$ 1 $\boxed{+}$ 864 $\boxed{\times}$ 0.04 $\boxed{+}$ 360 $\boxed{=}$
4. *A* = 365.76
5. 0.04 $\boxed{\div}$ 1 $\boxed{+}$ 1 $\boxed{\times}$ $\boxed{=}$ $\boxed{\times}$ 365.76 $\boxed{\div}$ $\boxed{=}$ $\boxed{=}$ $\boxed{\times}$ 360 $\boxed{\times}$ 20000 $\boxed{=}$
RTR: $18199.44

Thus, you have to invest $18199.44 at a rate (discount to yield) of 4% if you want to retrieve, in 864 days, a future value of $20000 (the rate being compounded annually).

Example: We want to retrieve $2815.14 860 days after having placed an unknown principal at 5% compounded quarterly. What is the principal?

1. 860 $\boxed{\times}$ 4 $\boxed{+}$ 360 $\boxed{=}$
2. *Y* = 9
3. 360 $\boxed{\times}$ 9 $\boxed{\div}$ 4 $\boxed{\times}$ $\boxed{-}$ 1 $\boxed{+}$ 860 $\boxed{\times}$ 0.05 $\boxed{+}$ 360 $\boxed{=}$
4. *A* = 362.5
5. 0.05 $\boxed{\div}$ 4 $\boxed{+}$ 1 $\boxed{\times}$ $\boxed{=}$ $\boxed{=}$ $\boxed{=}$ $\boxed{=}$ $\boxed{=}$ $\boxed{=}$ $\boxed{=}$ $\boxed{=}$ $\boxed{\times}$ 362.5 $\boxed{\div}$ $\boxed{=}$ $\boxed{=}$ $\boxed{\times}$ 360 $\boxed{\times}$ 2815.14 $\boxed{=}$
RTR = $2500 ($2499.98)

CHAPTER 10

ANNUITIES

An annuity is a series of equal payments made at equal periods of time. These payments can be made for two reasons: To accumulate capital, in which case the method is called *sinking fund;* or to reduce a loan, in which case the method is called *direct reduction of a loan.*

Payments can be made at the beginning or at the end of each period. However, in the case of the direct reduction loan, the payments are usually made at the end. In all cases the interest rate is compounded at the end of each period. Following are the various formulas:

Sinking Fund

Payments made *at the end* of each period.

$$F = A \left[\frac{(1 + i)^n - 1}{i} \right]$$

$$A = F \left[\frac{i}{(1 + i)^n - 1} \right]$$

Payments made *at the beginning* of each period.

$$F = A(1 + i)\left[\frac{(1 + i)^n - 1}{i}\right]$$

$$A = \frac{F}{(1 + i)\left[\frac{(1 + i)^n - 1}{i}\right]}$$

where F = Future value of capital
A = Payment
i = Rate (in decimal form) per period
n = Number of payments or periods.

DIRECT REDUCTION LOAN

Payments made at the end of each period

$$A = P\left[\frac{i}{1 - (1 + i)^{-n}}\right]$$

$$P = A\left[\frac{1 - (1 + i)^{-n}}{i}\right]$$

Where: P = Principal or loan, A = payment, i = Rate (decimal) per period, n = Number of periods (payments). (You might want to know that $a^{-n} = 1/a^n$).

Generalized Steps: Sinking Fund (Payments at End of Periods)

Future Value
 1. RATE $\boxed{\div}$ NUMBER OF PERIODS IN ONE YEAR $\boxed{=}$
 2. WTR = A

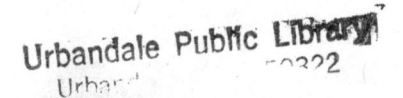

3. A ⊞ 1 ⊠ ⊟ ... (Press ⊟ a number of times equal to the number of periods or payments minus one) ⊟ 1 ⊞ A ⊠ PAYMENT ⊟ *Future Value*

Payment
1. RATE ⊞ NUMBER OF PERIODS PER YEAR ⊟
2. WTR = A
3. A ⊞ 1 ⊠ ⊟ ... (Press ⊟ a number of times equal to the number of payments minus one) ⊟ 1 ⊞ ⊟ ⊟ ⊠ A ⊠ FUTURE VALUE ⊟ *Payment*

Generalized Steps: Sinking Fund (Payments at Beginning of Periods)

Future Value
1. RATE ⊞ NUMBER OF PERIODS PER YEAR ⊟
2. WTR = A
3. A ⊞ 1 ⊠ ⊟ ... (Press ⊟ a number of times equal to the number of payments minus one) ⊟ 1 ⊞ A ⊠ PAYMENT ⊟
4. WTR = B
5. A ⊞ 1 ⊠ B ⊟ *Future Value*

Payment
1. RATE ⊞ NUMBER OF PERIODS PER YEAR ⊟
2. WTR = A
3. A ⊞ 1 ⊠ ⊟ ... (Press ⊟ a number of times equal to the number of payments minus one) ⊟ 1 ⊞ A ⊟
4. WTR = B
5. A ⊞ ⊠ B ⊞ ⊟ ⊟ ⊠ FUTURE VALUE ⊟ *Payment*

Example: How much capital will be accumulated if one deposits $100 at the end of each month for 12 months at 5%?
1. 0.05 ⊞ 12 ⊟
2. A = 0.00416

3. 0.00416 ⊞ 1 ⊠ ⊟ ⊟ ⊟ ⊟ ⊟ ⊟ ⊟ ⊟ ⊟ ⊟ ⊟
⊟ 1 ⊞ 0.00416 ⊠ 100 ⊟
RTR: $1227.87

Example: What payment does one have to deposit at the end of each of 12 months at 5% to accumulate $2000 in a year?
1. 0.05 ⊞ 12 ⊟
2. 0.00416 = A
3. 0.00416 ⊞ 1 ⊠ ⊟ ⊟ ⊟ ⊟ ⊟ ⊟ ⊟ ⊟ ⊟ ⊟ ⊟
⊟ 1 ⊞ ⊟ ⊟ ⊠ 2000 ⊠ 0.00416 ⊟
RTR: $162.88

Example: How much capital will be accumulated in a year if one deposits $100 at the beginning of each of 12 months at 5%?
1. 0.05 ⊞ 12 ⊟
2. 0.00416 = A
3. 0.00416 ⊞ 1 ⊠ ⊟ ⊟ ⊟ ⊟ ⊟ ⊟ ⊟ ⊟ ⊟ ⊟
⊟ ⊟ 1 ⊞ 0.00416 ⊠ 100 ⊟
4. 1227.8668 = B
5. 0.00416 ⊞ 1 ⊠ 1227.8668 ⊟
RTR: $1232.98

Example: What payment has to be deposited at the beginning of each of 12 months at 5% to retrieve capital of $2000 in a year?
1. 0.05 ⊞ 12 ⊟
2. 0.00416 = A
3. 0.00416 ⊞ 1 ⊠ ⊟ ⊟ ⊟ ⊟ ⊟ ⊟ ⊟ ⊟ ⊟ ⊟
⊟ 1 ⊞ 0.00416 ⊟
4. 12.278668 = B
5. 0.00416 ⊞ 1 ⊠ 12.278668 ⊞ ⊟ ⊟ ⊠ 2000 ⊟
RTR: $162.21

Generalized Steps: Direct Reduction Loan (Payments at End of Periods)

Payment
1. RATE ⊞ NUMBER OF PERIODS PER YEAR ⊟
2. WTR = A

Banking Problems

3. A [+] 1 [×] [=] ... (Press [=] a number of times equal to the number of payments minus one) [÷] [=] [=] [×] [−] 1 [+] 1 [÷] [=] [=] [×] A [×] PRINCIPAL [=]
Payment

Principal
1. RATE [÷] NUMBER OF PERIODS PER YEAR [=]
2. WTR = A
3. A [+] 1 [×] [=] ... (Press [=] a number of times equal to the number of payments minus one) [÷] [=] [=] [×] [−] 1 [+] 1 [÷] A [×] PAYMENT [=] *Principal*

Example: If you borrow $10000 at 13.38% and want to repay that loan in 36 months, what monthly payment is necessary?
1. 0.1338 [÷] 12 [=]
2. A = 0.01115
3. 0.01115 [+] 1 [×] [=] [+] [=] [=] [×] [−] 1 [+] 1 [÷] [=] [=] [×] 0.01115 [×] 10000 [=]
RTR: $338.77

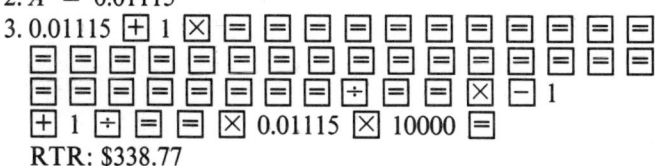

Example: What magnitude of loan can you expect to get from your bank if your budget will allow you to repay that loan in 10 quarterly payments of $500 at 12¼%.
1. 0.1225 [÷] 4 [=]
2. 0.030625 = A
3. 0.030625 [+] 1 [×] [=] [=] [=] [=] [=] [=] [=] [=] [=] [÷] [=] [=] [×] [−] 1 [+] 1 [÷] 0.030625 [×] 500 [=]
RTR: $4251.53

PART FOUR
STATISTICAL OPERATIONS

CHAPTER 11

THE MEANS

ARITHMETIC MEAN (also called AVERAGE)

If $a_1, a_2, a_3, \ldots, a_n$ are real numbers, then their arithmetic mean is

$$A = \frac{a_1 + a_2 + a_3 + \ldots + a_n}{n}, \text{ or } \frac{\Sigma a}{n}$$

For example, consider the following values: 2, 9, 12. (In this case, $a_1 = 2$; $a_2 = 9$; $a_3 = 12$, where $n = 3$.)

Their arithmetic mean is $(2 + 9 + 12)/3 = 7.\underline{6}$

Generalized Steps

Add all the values together and divide the sum by their number (n):

$$a_1 \boxplus a_2 \boxplus a_3 \boxplus \ldots \boxplus a_n \boxdiv n \boxminus \text{Mean}$$

In our example we did

$$2 \boxplus 9 \boxplus 12 \boxdiv 3 \boxminus \text{RTR: } 7.\underline{6}.$$

85

GEOMETRIC MEAN

If we consider a series of real numbers (all positive) $a_1, a_2, a_3, \ldots, a_n$, then their geometric mean is:

$$G = \sqrt[n]{a_1 \times a_2 \times a_3 \times \ldots \times a_n} \text{ or } \sqrt[n]{\Pi a}$$

Note that Π isn't π; Πa means "the product of all a's."

For example, consider the same series we had before: 2, 9, 12. Its geometric mean is $\sqrt[3]{2 \times 9 \times 12} = 6$.

Generalized Steps

1. Multiply all the values together:
   a_1 ☒ a_2 ☒ a_3 ☒ ... ☒ a_n ▣
2. WTR = A
3. A ⊞ NUMBER OF VALUES ▣
4. WTR = B
5. A ⊞ B ▣ (Depress ▣ a number of times equal to the number of values *minus one*)
6. ⊞ B ▣ (Same remark as in step (5))
7. ⊞ NUMBER OF VALUES ▣
8. WTR = B
9. GO TO STEP 5 using this "new B" and repeat steps 5 to 9 until two consecutive answers at step 8 are equal = Mean

For example, to solve our example, we do the following:
1. 2 ☒ 9 ☒ 12 ▣
2. A = 216
3. 216 ⊞ 3 ▣
4. B = 72
5. 216 ⊞ 72 ▣ ▣ (Twice since n = 3)
6. ⊞ 72 ▣ ▣ (ditto)
7. ⊞ 3 ▣
8. B = 48.013886
9. We go to step 5 with this "new B."

5. 216 $\boxed{+}$ 48.013886 $\boxed{=}$ $\boxed{=}$
6. $\boxed{+}$ 48.013886 $\boxed{=}$ $\boxed{=}$
7. $\boxed{\div}$ 3 $\boxed{=}$
8. $B = 32.040489$
9. We go to step 5 with this "new B."

5. 216 $\boxed{+}$ 32.040489 $\boxed{=}$ $\boxed{=}$
6. $\boxed{+}$ 32.040489 $\boxed{=}$ $\boxed{=}$
7. $\boxed{\div}$ 3 $\boxed{=}$
8. $B = 21.43046$
9. We go to step 5 with this "new B" ... and so on.
You will get as "new B": 14.443745
9.9742853
7.3732403
6.2398826
6.0091033
6.0000133

and then twice 5.9999996, which is equivalent to 6 (the answer).

HARMONIC MEAN

$$H = \frac{n}{\dfrac{1}{a_1} + \dfrac{1}{a_2} + \dfrac{1}{a_3} + \ldots + \dfrac{1}{a_n}}$$

Generalized Steps

1. Compute the reciprocal of each value
   a_1 $\boxed{\div}$ $\boxed{=}$ $\boxed{=}$ a_2 $\boxed{\div}$ $\boxed{=}$ $\boxed{=}$ ... etc.
2. WTR of each reciprocal = B_1 B_2 ... etc.
3. Add all the reciprocals:
   B_1 $\boxed{+}$ B_2 $\boxed{+}$ ... $\boxed{+}$ $\boxed{=}$ $\boxed{=}$ $\boxed{\times}$ NUMBER OF VALUES
   $\boxed{=}$ *Mean*

Example: 3, 5, 6
1. 3 $\boxed{\div}$ $\boxed{=}$ $\boxed{=}$ 5 $\boxed{\div}$ $\boxed{=}$ $\boxed{=}$ 6 $\boxed{\div}$ $\boxed{=}$ $\boxed{=}$
2. $B_1 = 0.\underline{3}$ $B_2 = 0.2$ $B_3 = 0.1\underline{6}$

3. 0.$\underline{3}$ ⊞ 0.2 ⊞ 0.1$\underline{6}$ ⊞ ⊟ ⊟ ⊠ 3 ⊟
RTR: 4.2857148

The relationship of each of these three means is:
arithmetic mean ⩾ geometric mean ⩾ harmonic mean.

THE MEDIAN

The middle value of a series of values if their number is odd, or the arithmetic mean of the two middle values if their number is even, is called the *median*. For example, in 1, 2, $\boxed{3}$, 6, 7, the number of values = 5 = odd; hence the median is 3. In the example of 1, 2, $\boxed{3, 6,}$ 7, 10, the number of values = 6 = even; hence the median is the arithmetic mean of 3 and 6:

3 ⊞ 6 ⊞ 2 ⊟   RTR: 4.5

THE MODE

The value X_m having a maximum frequency F_m is the mode. Consider this sample:

2, 2, 2, 3, 3, 4, 4, 4, 4, 4, 5, 5, 6, 6, 6, 8, 12

There are three 2's; two 3's; five 4's; two 5's; three 6's; one 8; one 12. The mode is then 4 since this value has the highest frequency in the series.

X_m	F_m
2	3
3	2
④	5←
5	2
6	3
8	1
12	1

CHAPTER 12

LINEAR REGRESSION

The least squares method permits one to construct a straight line through a group of points where the distances between each point and the line are at a minimum in order to represent a *trend line*, from which one can derive useful statistical information. Linear regression methods are used typically for projecting events based upon the extrapolation from a known trend. This can be best demonstrated on a graph (Fig. 12.1), where the line X (or X-axis), called the *abscissa*, is horizontal and the line Y (or Y-axis), called the *ordinate*, is vertical and usually meets the X-axis at zero. Both of these lines are scaled.

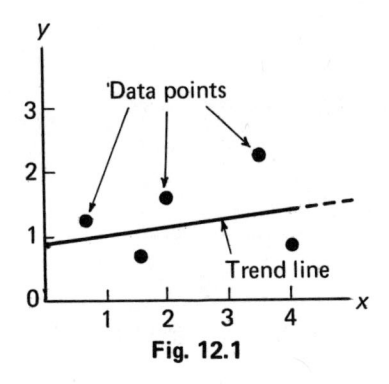

Fig. 12.1

You can often see such graphs in the business section of a newspaper. The Dow Jones Industrial Average, for example, is charted on a graph where the X-axis represents the scale of time (days or weeks) and the Y-axis represents a scale of values. In such a graph it is possible to determine what value the Dow Jones had at a precise point in time.

A data point is a graphical representation of two coordinates. A few examples of what these coordinates can be are as follows: time and value; time and temperature; time and profit (or deficit) of a company; amount of chemical added to a batch and final concentration of the chemical in the final product; and so on. These are algebraically notated (X, Y). The time, as an example, can be represented by the coordinate X, and the value then is represented by the coordinate Y. This method of representation of data as a point or group of points on a graph can use various coordinate systems; in this book we shall consider only the rectangular Cartesian coordinates system. In this system the X coordinate of the system (X, Y) indicates that the point is situated on a perpendicular that reaches the X-axis at the value X. The Y coordinate, in turn, indicates that the point is situated on a perpendicular that reaches the Y-axis at the value Y. The point is thereby defined at the intersection of these two perpendiculars. For example, the point (3, 2) where $X = 3$ and $Y = 2$ is graphed as in Fig. 12.2.

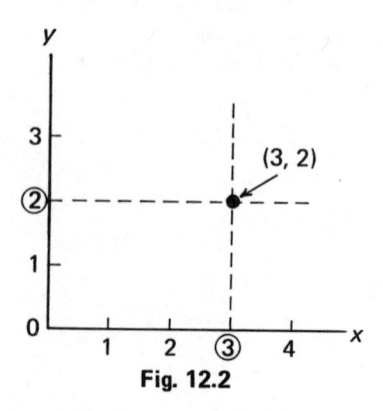

Fig. 12.2

The points (1, 3) and (4, 2) are graphed in Fig. 12.3.

Statistical Operations

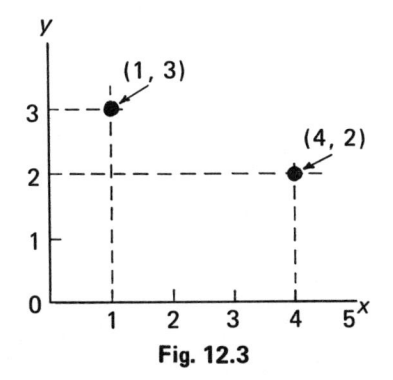

Fig. 12.3

Remember that the first coordinate in the system (a, b) represents the value X and that the second coordinate represents Y.

In the same manner that an algebraic equation should always be accompanied by the definition of each letter, the scales of a graph (the scales on the X-axis and Y-axis) should always be defined.

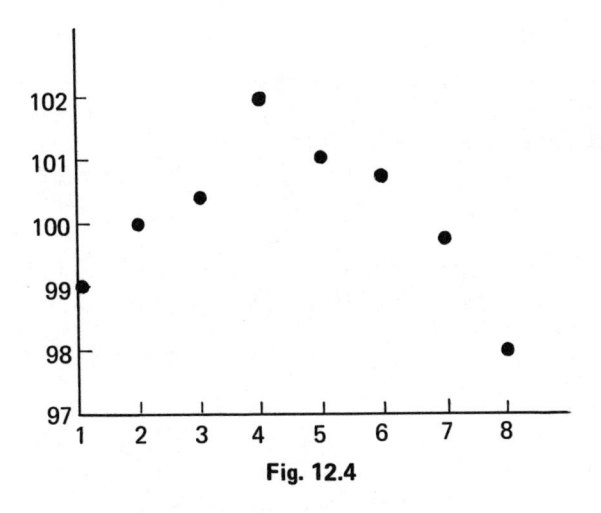

Fig. 12.4

Indeed, the graph in Fig. 12.4 is meaningless, but that in Fig.

12.5 is meaningful and is easily interpreted.

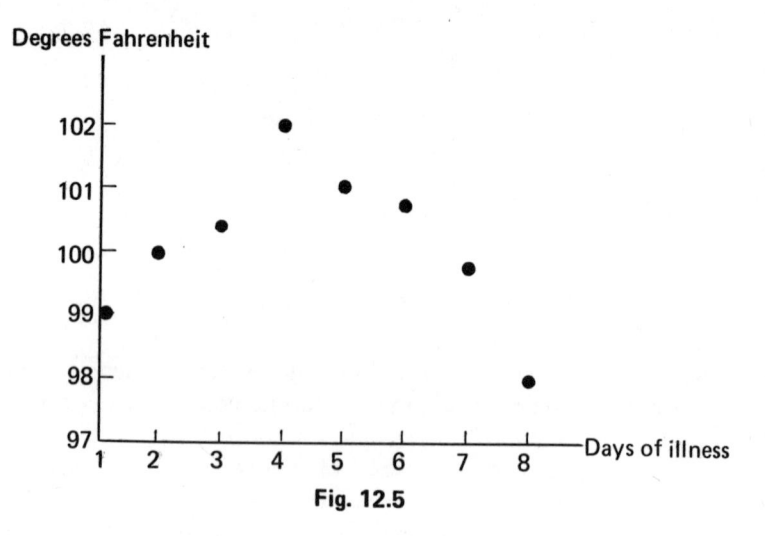

Degrees Fahrenheit

Fig. 12.5

THE STRAIGHT LINE

This equation of the straight line allows us to compute the coordinates of any point we choose on the trend line—that is, to establish projections without even drawing a graph. The equation of the straight line is written

$$Y = a \cdot X + b$$

where X and Y are the Cartesian coordinates of a point (X, Y) that is situated on the line: a is called the *slope* of the line and b is called the *Y-intercept* of the line.

Don't be frightened by these strange names; it is in fact very simple. Once we have (computed) a and b on the basis of past events, we will be able to replace or "inject" a known quantity in place of X and thus get a "projected Y" (unknown).

Let's take an example: A businessman has the following sales figures for the last six years and wants to forecast his

Statistical Operations

theoretical sales figures for the next six years based on the trend line of the first six years' sales.

Years	Sales ($ in thousand)
1	250
2	300
3	350
4	350
5	300
6	400

These six sales figures can be graphed as in Fig. 12.6, to attribute the time (years) to the X-axis and the sales ($) to the Y-axis.

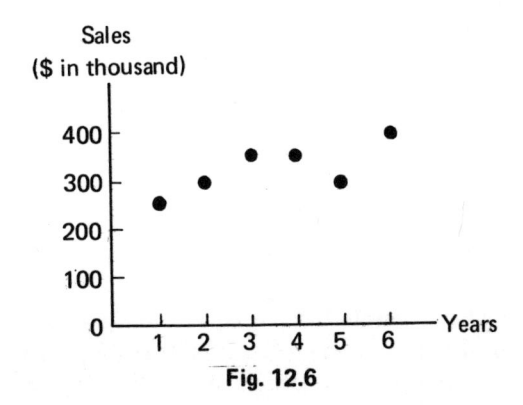

Fig. 12.6

We now want to draw a trend line through these points in order to forecast sales for the next six years. To do so we compute the equation of that line (the method will be shown later on) and get

$$Y = 21.428571 \cdot X + 250$$

where $a = 21.428571$ and $b = 250$. Replace X by any value (let's take 7) and compute Y.

7 ☒ 21.428571 ⊞ 250 ⊟   RTR: 400

Thus we have defined one point on the trend line. This first point is (7,400).

We take another value for X and compute Y; (this time lets take $X = 0$). Since any value multiplied by zero equals zero, we have defined our second point as being (0, 250).

Verify: 0 $\boxed{\times}$ 21.428571 $\boxed{+}$ 250 $\boxed{=}$ RTR: 250

With the coordinates of these two points we are now able to draw the trend line through the data points already on the graph (see Fig. 12.7).

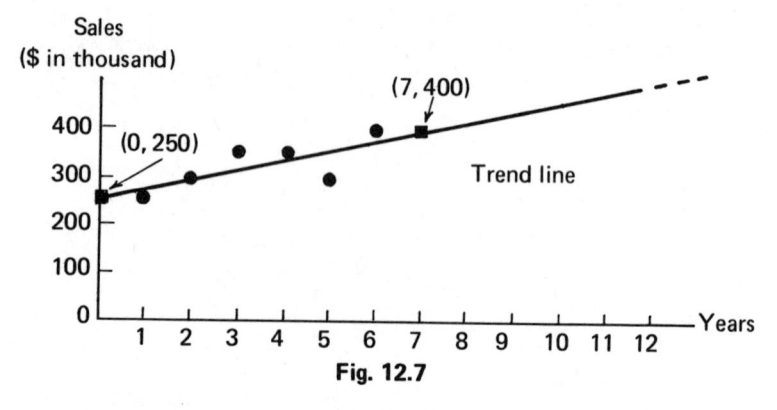

Fig. 12.7

The trend line meets the Y-axis at the figure 250. This is why the b in the trend line equation is called Y-intercept. For the mathematically inclined reader, the a of our equation is the tangent (a trigonometric term) of the angle formed at the intersection of the trend line and the X-axis. This is why a is called the "slope" of the line. (Don't worry, you do not need to understand this to use this linear regression method.)

The first of the "next six years" is year number seven, since the trend is based on the figures of the years numbered one to six. Since we attributed the time (years) to the X-axis, X will be replaced in our equation of the trend line by the number of a year and Y will give us a sales figure in thousands of dollars.

Thus our equation is $Y = 21.428571 X + 250$. We replace X by 7 and get $Y = 21.428571 \cdot 7 + 250$.

Statistical Operations

We compute:

21.428571 ☒ 7 ⊞ 250 ⊟   RTR: 399.9 = 400

Now this result is the same as the second coordinate we computed in order to draw the trend line. This result (400) means that during the seventh year the businessman should theoretically sell $400,000 worth of merchandise.

To find the projected sales for the eighth year (or second year after the first series of six years) we replace X by 8 and compute:

21.428571 ☒ 8 ⊞ 250 ⊟   RTR: 421.42856

This means that during the eighth year the sales should theoretically amount to $421428.56. Call it $421,000.

The ninth year:

21.428571 ☒ 9 ⊞ 250 ⊟   RTR: 442.85713

In dollars, that's about $443,000.

We are now able to create the following table:

Years	Sales
	(Actual)
1	250,000
2	300,000
3	350,000
4	350,000
5	300,000
6	400,000
	(Projected)
7	400,000
8	421,000
9	443,000
10	464,000
11	486,000
12	507,000

Had we drawn a dotted line on the graph perpendicular to the Fig. 12.7 on the X-axis (Years scale), we would have met the trend line at a point perpendicular to the figure 400 on the scale of the sales (Y-axis).

The same applies for the following years: a dotted line leaving the X-axis at 8 would meet the trend line at a point directly opposite the figure 421 on the Y-axis and so on. These points, which are on the trend line, have the following coordinates: (7, 400); (8, 421); (9, 443); (10, 464); (11, 486); and (12, 507).

THE TREND LINE

We shall now demonstrate how to compute the a and the b of the equation of the trend line:

$$Y = aX + b$$

First, a word of warning: When you want to compute a linear regression, it is imperative to decide at the beginning what result you expect from your calculation—that is, what the X and the Y in the equation will stand for. In our example the X was the number of a year and Y was a sales figure in thousands of dollars.

In general you must choose your X as a quantity you will be able to "inject" easily in the equation (once you know the value of a and b) in order to get the "projected Y." In our example we expected to get an unknown projected sales figure from a known point in time (seventh, eighth year, etc. ...). This is why we decided to inject the number of a year in place of X; this quantity was indeed easily determined. The X became the coordinate of time (in years) and the Y the coordinate of sales (in dollars).

Now that we have decided what X and Y stand for, we have to draw a table for the available sales figures.

Statistical Operations

Years (X)	Sales (in thousands of dollars) (Y)
1	250
2	300
3	350
4	350
5	300
6	400

This table is now enlarged and filled out in such a way as to prepare the computation of *a* and *b*.

n	X^2	X	Y	XY
		1	250	
		2	300	
		3	350	
		4	350	
		5	300	
		6	400	
TOTALS				

In the *n* column we simply count the number of data lines (sales figures by year) we have and write the result. In this case $n = 6$, since we have six figures for six years.

n	X^2	X	Y	XY
		1	250	
		2	300	
6		3	350	
		4	350	
		5	300	
		6	400	
TOTALS				

In the X^2 column, we "square" each X; that is, we multiply each X by itself. Compute:

(1 ☒ ☲)   WTR: 1
 2 ☒ ☲   WTR: 4
 3 ☒ ☲   WTR: 9
 4 ☒ ☲   WTR: 16
 5 ☒ ☲   WTR: 25
 6 ☒ ☲   WTR: 36

Then we add all these results and write their sum in the proper place below:

n	X^2	X	Y	XY
6	1	1	250	
	4	2	300	
	9	3	350	
	16	4	350	
	25	5	300	
	36	6	400	
TOTALS	91			

Now, add all the X's and write their sum in its proper place. Do the same for all Y's.

n	X^2	X	Y	XY
6	1	1	250	
	4	2	300	
	9	3	350	
	16	4	350	
	25	5	300	
	36	6	400	
TOTALS	91	21	1950	

Statistical Operations

In the XY column we inscribe the product of each pair of X's and Y's and add all the results, writing the various results in their proper places. (Here a cumulative memory saves the time spent adding the various sums together.)

(1 ☒ 250 ☒)   WTR: 250
2 ☒ 300 ☒   WTR: 600
3 ☒ 350 ☒   WTR: 1050
4 ☒ 350 ☒   WTR: 1400
5 ☒ 300 ☒   WTR: 1500
6 ☒ 400 ☒   WTR: 2400
250 ☒ 600 ☒ 1050 ☒ 1400 ☒ 1500 ☒ 2400 ☒
WTR: 7200

n	X^2	X	Y	XY
	1	1	250	250
	4	2	300	600
6	9	3	350	1050
	16	4	350	1400
	25	5	300	1500
	36	6	400	2400
TOTALS	91	21	1950	7200

A sum, in algebra, is notated by the Greek letter sigma—Σ. Hence the sums or totals we have are written:

$$n = 6$$
$$\Sigma X^2 = 91$$
$$\Sigma X = 21$$
$$\Sigma Y = 1950$$
$$\Sigma XY = 7200$$

The following formulas are now introduced:

$$a = \frac{(n\Sigma XY) - (\Sigma X \Sigma Y)}{(n\Sigma X^2) - (\Sigma X)^2}$$

$$b = \frac{(\Sigma Y \Sigma X^2) - (\Sigma X \Sigma X Y)}{(n\Sigma X^2) - (\Sigma X)^2}$$

With the results we now have, they become:

$$a = \frac{(6 \times 7200) - (21 \times 1950)}{(6 \times 91) - (21)(21)}$$

$$b = \frac{(1950 \times 91) - (21 \times 7200)}{(6 \times 91) - (21)(21)}$$

We compute:

6 ×7200 =	WTR: 43200	= $n\Sigma XY$
21 × 1950 =	WTR: 40950	= $\Sigma X \Sigma Y$
6 × 91 =	WTR: 546	= $n\Sigma X^2$
21 × 21 =	WTR: 441	= $(\Sigma X)^2$
1950 × 91 =	WTR: 177450	= $\Sigma Y \Sigma X^2$
21 × 7200 =	WTR: 151200	= $\Sigma X \Sigma X Y$

The equations can now be written:

$$a = \frac{43200 - 40950}{546 - 441}$$

$$b = \frac{177450 - 151200}{546 - 441}$$

Computing the denominators

546 − 441 =

and noting 105, we get a with

43200 − 40950 ÷ 105 =   WTR: a = 21.428571

Statistical Operations

We get *b* with

177450 ⊟ 151200 ⊞ 105 ⊟   WTR: $b = 250$

We are finally able to write the equation:

$$Y = 21.428571\ X + 250$$

Once you have the equation of the trend line, it is the simplest thing to calculate any "projected *Y*" by inserting any quantity in place of *X* (in general, the rank of a day, week, month, semester, year, etc. ...). Simply multiply *X* by *a* and add *b* to the product to find *Y*.

X ⊠ a ⊞ b ⊟   RTR: Y

Here is another example of a linear regression. Our businessman, this time not as successful, is confronted with the following sales figures for a period of four years.

Years	Sales (in thousand of dollars)
1	350
2	400
3	250
4	300

On the basis of these figures he wants to compute a trend line and project theoretical sales figures for the next two years. First we create our table and compute its various components:

n	X^2	X	Y	XY
	1	1	350	350
	4	2	400	800
4	9	3	250	750
	16	4	300	1200
TOTALS	30	10	1300	3100
	ΣX^2	ΣX	ΣY	ΣXY

Introducing the formulas for *a* and *b*, we write

$$a = \frac{(4 \times 3100) - (10 \times 1300)}{(4 \times 30) - (10)(10)}$$

$$b = \frac{(1300 \times 30) - (10 \times 3100)}{(4 \times 30) - (10)(10)}$$

We compute the various products in order to eliminate the parentheses:

$$a = \frac{12400 - 13000}{120 - 100}$$

$$b = \frac{39000 - 3100}{120 - 100}$$

We establish the denominators:

120 ⊟ 100 ⊟   WTR: 20

a is retrieved with

12400 ⊟ 13000 ⊞ 20 ⊟   RTR: −30

b is retrieved with

39000 ⊟ 31000 ⊞ 20 ⊟   RTR: 400

The question has thus become $Y = -30X + 400$.

The fifth year's sales projection is then easily computed:

⊟ 30 ⊠ 5 ⊞ 400 ⊟   RTR: 250 (250,000 dollars)

The sixth year's projection:

⊟ 30 ⊠ 6 ⊞ 400 ⊟   RTR: 220 (220,000 dollars)

Statistical Operations

Note that a (the slope of the trend line) is negative, and indeed the sales figures are dropping, to the despair of our businessman. In the chart for the values we now have (Fig. 12.8) we see the trend line dropping to the right.

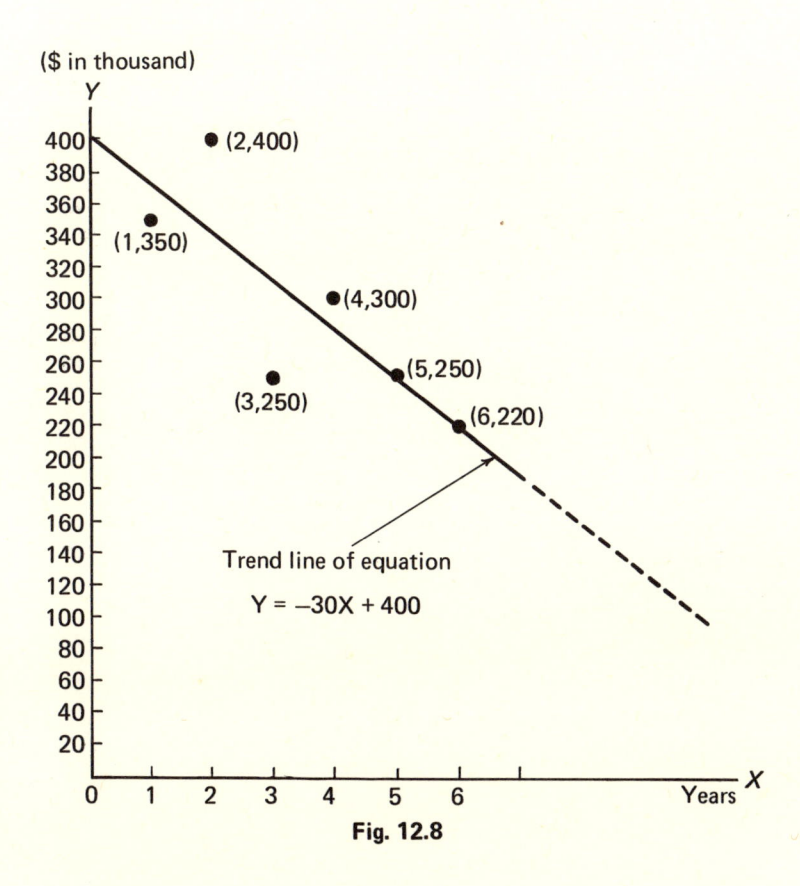

($ in thousand)

Trend line of equation
$Y = -30X + 400$

Fig. 12.8

If the businessman wanted to know at what year his sales figures would theoretically be zero, we would then transform our trend line equation in order to get the X (year), and not the Y, alone on one side of the equal sign. To do this a little algebra is necessary:

$Y = aX + b$ is the equation of the trend line

$Y - b = aX$ b is shifted to the left side

$$\frac{Y - b}{a} = X \quad a \text{ is shifted left, too, isolating } X$$

Perhaps it should be explained what happened here. We started with the common equation of the trend line, $Y = aX + b$. Since one is allowed to perform any operation on one side of an equation, provided the same operation is performed on its other side, we first subtracted b from each side:

$$Y - b = aX + b - b$$

We simplify:

$$Y - b = aX \not{+ b} \not{- b}$$

and get $Y - b = aX$. We then divided each side by a:

$$\frac{Y - b}{a} = \frac{aX}{a}$$

We simplify:

$$\frac{Y - b}{a} = \frac{\not{a}X}{\not{a}}$$

and get

$$\frac{Y - b}{a} = X$$

So we have $X = (Y - b)/a$, and since $a = -30$ and $b = 400$, we write:

$$X = \frac{Y - 400}{-30}$$

Remember that Y is the sales in dollars. In this case Y is equal to zero (no sales), and so we write:

$$X = \frac{0 - 400}{-30}$$

Compute:

$\boxed{-}$ 400 $\boxed{\div}$ $\boxed{-}$ 30 $\boxed{=}$ RTR: 13.$\underline{3}$

(The depression of the "zero" key before the $\boxed{-}$ key isn't necessary.) This means that our unfortunate businessman would theoretically be in very bad shape during the course of the fourteenth year (ten years after he had computed his trend line). This example thus illustrates the very theoretical aspect of such an analysis.

The method of establishing how well a linear regression, or trend line, fits the data on which it is based is called *coefficient of determination*. It is notated as r^2. If the trend line fits the data perfectly, r^2 will equal one. If there is no fit, r^2 will equal zero, in which case the projection has no practical value at all.

The computation of the coefficient of determination is a bit tedious with a common calculator, but we will nevertheless include a method for its calculation here. First consider the following:

Generalized Steps: Trend Line Equation

1. Decide what X and Y will stand for (usually X represents a time period).
2. Create a table with the X's and Y's facing each other on a one-to-one correspondence.
3. Count the number of (X, Y) pairs in the table.
4. WTR: n
5. Square every X—that is, multiply each X by itself

once—and then add all the results to get the sum of all the squares.
6. WTR: A
7. Multiply each X by the corresponding Y, and add all the results (products) to get the sum of the products.
8. WTR: D
9. Add all the X's
10. WTR: B
11. Add all the Y's
12. WTR: C
13. Compute: n ☒ D ☐
14. WTR: E
15. Compute: B ☒ C ☐
16. WTR: F
17. Compute: n ☒ A ☐
18. WTR: G
19. Compute: B ☒ B ☐ *or* simply: B ☒ ☐
20. WTR: H
21. Compute: C ☒ A ☐
22. WTR: J
23. Compute: B ☒ D ☐
24. WTR: K
25. Compute: G ☐ H ☐
26. WTR: L
27. Compute: E ☐ F ☐ L ☐
28. WTR: a
29. Compute: J ☐ K ☐ L ☐
30. WTR: b
31. Write the trend line equation with the a and b you got at steps 28 and 30.

$$Y = aX + b$$

32. Compute a projected Y by replacing X with the quantity of your choice (usually the rank of a time period—i.e., 5th month, 3rd year, 4th quarter etc. ...) with

Statistical Operations 107

$$X \boxtimes a \boxplus b \boxminus$$

and read the *answer* or "projected *Y*."
33. To compute yet another projected *Y*, go back to step 32 with another *X*.

COEFFICIENT OF DETERMINATION (r²)

Figs. 12.9–12.12 are a few graphic examples to illustrate its use:

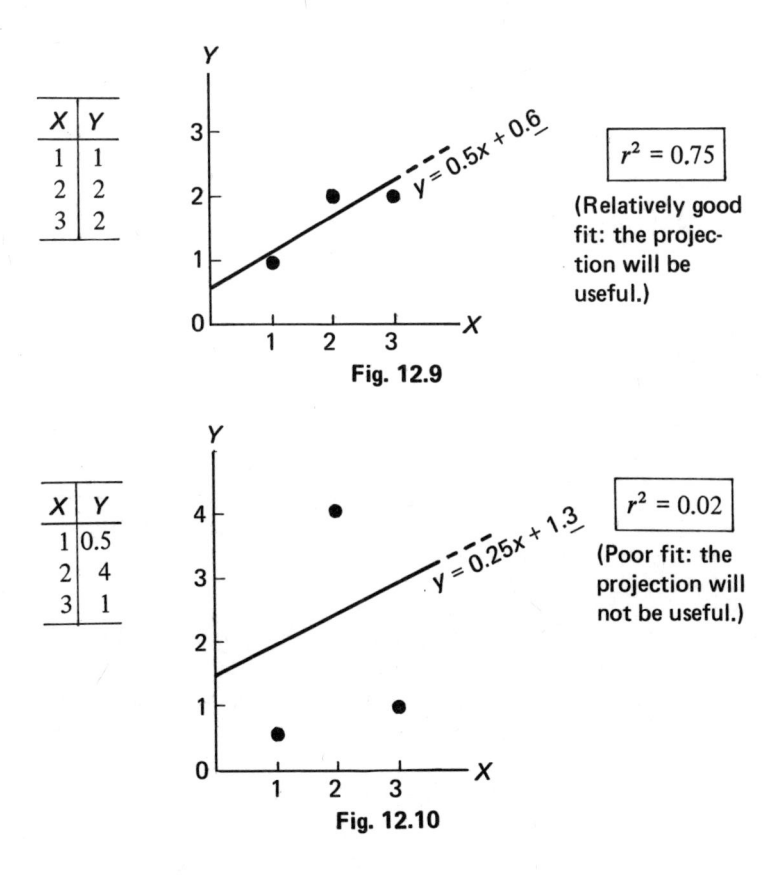

X	Y
1	1
2	2
3	2

$y = 0.5x + 0.6$

$r^2 = 0.75$

(Relatively good fit: the projection will be useful.)

Fig. 12.9

X	Y
1	0.5
2	4
3	1

$y = 0.25x + 1.3$

$r^2 = 0.02$

(Poor fit: the projection will not be useful.)

Fig. 12.10

X	Y
1	2
2	3
3	4

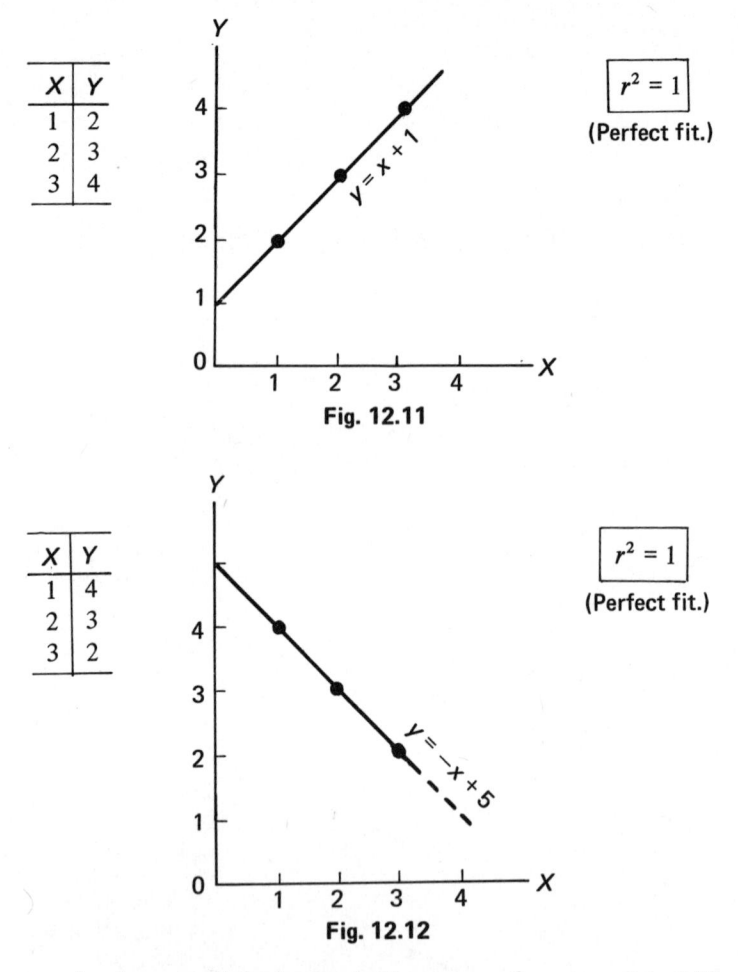

$r^2 = 1$
(Perfect fit.)

Fig. 12.11

X	Y
1	4
2	3
3	2

$r^2 = 1$
(Perfect fit.)

Fig. 12.12

In the case of the happy businessman r^2 was equal to 0.58. In the case of the unhappy businessman $r^2 = 0.36$, which could mean that the fortunate businessman had a better reason to be happy than his competitor had to be unhappy. (See p. 112.)

Generalized Steps: Coefficient of Determination

Of especial interest to the mathematically inclined is the formula for this procedure:

Statistical Operations

$$r^2 = \frac{[\Sigma(X - \bar{X})(Y - \bar{Y})]}{[\Sigma(X - \bar{X})^2][\Sigma(Y - \bar{Y})^2]}$$

where r^2 is the coefficient of determination
$\bar{X}$ is the arithmetic mean (or average) of all Y's
$\bar{Y}$ is the arithmetic mean (or average) of all Y's.

1. Create a table with the X's and the Y's facing each other on a one-to-one correspondence.
2. Count the number of (X, Y) pairs in the table.
3. WTR: n
4. Add all the X's and divide their sum by n.
5. WTR: $\bar{X}$
6. Add all the Y's and divide their sum by n.
7. WTR: $\bar{Y}$
8. Subtract $\bar{X}$ from the first X; X_1 ⊟ $\bar{X}$ ⊟
9. WTR: A_1
10. Subtract $\bar{X}$ from the second X and so on:

X_2 ⊟ $\bar{X}$ ⊟ X_3 ⊟ $\bar{X}$ ⊟ etc. ....

11. WTR: A_2 ... A_3 ... A_4 etc. ....
12. Perform steps 10 and 11 until all X's have been "treated."
13. Subtract $\bar{Y}$ from the first Y.
14. WTR: B_1
15. Subtract $\bar{Y}$ from the second ... third ... fourth Y, etc. ....
16. WTR: B_2 ... B_3 ... B_4 etc. ....
17. Perform steps 15 and 16 until all Y's have been "treated."
18. Multiply the first A by the first B:

A_1 ⊠ B_1 ⊟

19. WTR: C_1
20. Multiply the second A by the second B and so on ....

A_2 ⊠ B_2 ⊟ A_3 ⊠ B_3 ⊟ etc. ....

21. WTR: C_2 ... C_3 ... C_4 etc. ....
22. Perform steps 20 and 21 until all A's and B's (having the same subscript) have been multiplied.
23. Add all the C's together:

$$C_1 \boxplus C_2 \boxplus \ldots \boxplus C_n \boxminus$$

24. WTR: D
25. Compute:

$$D \boxtimes D \boxminus \quad or \quad D \boxtimes \boxminus$$

26. WTR: E
27. Multiply each A by itself starting with A_1, A_2, etc. ..., until all A's have been squared.
28. WTR: F_1 ... F_2 ... F_3 etc. ....
29. Perform step 27 for all B's until all B's have been squared.
30. WTR: G_1 ... G_2 ... G_3 ... G_4 etc. ...
31. Add all the G's together:

$$G_1 \boxplus G_2 \boxplus \ldots \boxplus G_n \boxminus$$

32. WTR: H
33. Add all F's together.
34. WTR: J.
35. Compute:

$$E \boxplus H \boxplus J \boxminus$$

36. RTR: *Answer* r^2

Again remember that the closer the answer is to 1 the better the trend line fits the points (data) and thus can be used to yield valuable projections.

Example: Following is the procedure to compute the coefficient of determination of a trend line based on these data: (1, 1) (2, 2) (3, 2)

1. | X | Y |
    |---|---|
    | 1 | 1 |
    | 2 | 2 |
    | 3 | 2 |

2. There are three pairs of X's and Y's
3. $n = 3$
4. 1 $\boxplus$ 2 $\boxplus$ 3 $\boxplus$ 3 $\boxminus$
5. $\bar{X} = 2$
6. 1 $\boxplus$ 2 $\boxplus$ 2 $\boxplus$ 3 $\boxminus$
7. $\bar{Y} = 1.\underline{6}$
8. 1 $\boxminus$ 2 $\boxminus$
9. $A_1 = -1$
10-12. 2 $\boxminus$ (using the constant in step 8)
    3 $\boxminus$ $A_2 = 0$ $A_3 = 1$
13. 1 $\boxminus$ 1.6
14. $B_1 = -0.\underline{6}$
15-17. 2 $\boxminus$ (using the constant set in step 13)
    2 $\boxminus$ $B_2 = 0.\underline{3}$ $B_3 = 0.\underline{3}$
18. $\boxminus$ 1 $\boxtimes$ $\boxminus$ 0.6 $\boxminus$
19. $C_1 = 0.\underline{6}$
20-22. We know that the product of any figure multiplied by zero is zero and that the product of any figure multiplied by one is that figure. Hence $C_2 = 0$, $C_3 = 0.\underline{3}$
    0.$\underline{3}$
23. 0.$\underline{6}$ $\boxplus$ 0.$\underline{3}$ $\boxminus$
24. $D = 1$
25. (1 $\boxtimes$ 1 $\boxminus$) (same remark as in step 22)
26. $E = 1$
27-28. $\boxminus$ 1 $\boxtimes$ $\boxminus$ 1 $\boxminus$
    (same remark as in step 20)

    $F_1 = 1$
    $F_2 = 0$
    $F_3 = 1$
29-30. $\boxminus$ 0.$\underline{6}$ $\boxtimes$ 0.$\underline{6}$ $\boxminus$
    0.$\underline{3}$ $\boxtimes$ 0.$\underline{3}$ $\boxminus$
    ditto
    $G_1 = 0.\underline{4}$
    $G_2 = 0.\underline{1}$
    $G_3 = 0.\underline{1}$
31. 0.$\underline{4}$ $\boxplus$ 0.$\underline{1}$ $\boxplus$ 0.$\underline{1}$ $\boxminus$

32. $H = 0.\underline{6}$
33. 1 ⊞ 1 ⊟
34. $J = 2$
35. 1 ⊞ 0.$\underline{6}$ ⊞ 2 ⊟
36. *answer:* $r^2 = 0.75$

Compare this result with the coefficient of determination given with the first graphic example at the beginning of this chapter (p. 107, Fig. 12.9).

Example: What is the coefficient of determination of the trend line based on the following data?

(1. 350); (2, 400); (3, 250); (4, 300).

(These points are identical to the sales figures of our unhappy businessman.)

1.

X	Y
1	350
2	400
3	250
4	300

2. and 3. $n = 4$
4. 1 ⊞ 2 ⊞ 3 ⊞ 4 ⊡ 4 ⊟
5. $\bar{X} = 2.5$
6. 350 ⊞ 400 ⊞ 250 ⊞ 300 ⊡ 4 ⊟
7. $\bar{Y} = 325$
8-12. 1 ⊟ 2.5 ⊟ $A_1 = -1.5$
      2 ⊟ (constant) $A_2 = -0.5$
      3 ⊟ $A_3 = 0.5$
      4 ⊟ $A_4 = 1.5$
13-17. 350 ⊟ 325 ⊟ $B_1 = 25$
       400 ⊟ (constant) $B_2 = 75$
       250 ⊟ $B_3 = -75$
       300 ⊟ $B_4 = -25$
18-22. ⊟ 1.5 ⊠ 25 ⊟ $C_1 = -37.5$
       ⊟ 0.5 ⊠ 75 ⊟ $C_2 = -37.5$
       0.5 ⊠ ⊟ 75 ⊟ $C_3 = -37.5$
       1.5 ⊠ ⊟ 25 ⊟ $C_4 = -37.5$

Statistical Operations

23. $\boxed{-}$ 37.5 $\boxed{\times}$ 4 $\boxed{=}$ (which is quicker)
24. $D = -150$
25. $\boxed{-}$ 150 $\boxed{\times}$ $\boxed{=}$
26. $E = 22500$
27. to 28. $\boxed{-}$ 1.5 $\boxed{\times}$ $\boxed{=}$
    $\boxed{-}$ 0.5 $\boxed{\times}$ $\boxed{=}$ hence $F_1 = 2.25$
    $F_2 = 0.25$
    $F_3 = 0.25$
    $F_4 = 2.25$

29-30. 25 $\boxed{\times}$ $\boxed{=}$
    75 $\boxed{\times}$ $\boxed{=}$ hence $G_1 = 625$
    $G_2 = 5625$
    $G_3 = 5625$
    $G_4 = 625$

31. 625 $\boxed{+}$ 5625 $\boxed{+}$ 5625 $\boxed{+}$ 625 $\boxed{=}$
32. $H = 12500$
33. 2.25 $\boxed{+}$ 0.25 $\boxed{+}$ 0.25 $\boxed{+}$ 2.25 $\boxed{=}$
34. $J = 5$
35. 22500 $\boxed{\div}$ 12500 $\boxed{\div}$ 5 $\boxed{=}$
36. *answer:* $r^2 = 0.36$

This coefficient, as we have said, is rather low, which should tranquilize our businessman—a little.

CHAPTER 13

PROBABILITY

This chapter may help you earn a bit playing cards, dice, roulette, and similar games—or it could very well persuade you that it is wiser to play chess!

Probability is used to determine whether one or more *future* events is

> impossible
> improbable
> plausible
> certain

(with an infinite range between impossible and certain).

Usually the probability of the outcome of an event is notated p_E. This probability has the range $0 \leqslant p_E \leqslant 1$. If $p_E = 0$, the probability that the event E will happen is nil—that is, the event E is impossible. If $p_E = 1$, on the other hand, the event E is certain to happen. (If you multiply p_E by 100, you can use that figure ($100p_E = N$) to say "There are N chances in a hundred for the event E to happen.")

SIMPLE PROBABILITY

If a given event E can occur in m different ways, out of a total of n possibilities, all equally likely, the probability of E is m/n and is notated:

$$p_E = \frac{m}{n}$$

Again, the closer p_E comes to 1, the more the event is likely to happen. Let's take two examples: First, what is the probability for an "ace" to turn up when a six-sided die is thrown once? The ace can turn up in only one way out of a total of six possible. Hence $m = 1$ and $n = 6$. We have then 1/6; thus $p_E = 0.1\underline{6}$.

The second example determines the probability of drawing a jack when a card is chosen at random in an ordinary deck of 52 cards. Since there are four jacks in a deck, there are 4 chances in 52. Here $m = 4$ and $n = 52$. Thus, $p_E = 4/52 = 0.076923\underline{0}$.

If the probability of an event E is p_E, p_E is also called the *probability of success* of E. The probability of "failure" of E is 1 $- p_E$. We write:

$$p_{\not{E}} = 1 - p_E$$

Going back to our two examples, first we can determine the probability that an "ace" will *not* turn up. (In other words, what is the probability of a two or a three or a four or a five or a six turning up in a single trial?) Since p_E for the ace is $0.1\underline{6}$, $p_{\not{E}}$ is

1 ⊟ 0.1\underline{6} ⊟   RTR: 0.8\underline{3}

Second, what is the probability of drawing a card that is not a jack when one card is chosen at random in a deck of 52?

$$p_E \text{ for one jack} = \frac{4}{52};$$

$$p_{\not{E}} = 1 - \frac{4}{52} = \frac{48}{52} = 0.92307\underline{6}$$

Check: 4 ⊞ 52 ⊠ ⊟ 1 ⊞ 1 ⊟   RTR: 0.9230770

If p_E is the probability that a person will win a sum of C dollars, then $\$Cp_E$ is called his *expectation*.

Example: John will win $5 if he draws a red ball from a bag containing 3 black balls and 2 red balls. What is his *expectation*? The bag contains 5 balls; thus he has 2 chances in 5 of drawing a red ball: $m = 2$; $n = 5$; $C = \$5$. Hence, $p_E = 2/5 = 0.4$. His expectation is thus $p_E \times C\$$

0.4 ⊠ 5 ⊟   RTR: 2

The answer is two dollars.

Example: If you play at French roulette (where there are 36 numbers plus one zero), what is your expectation if you bet $10 once on one number? In this case $m = 1$; $n = 37$; and $C = \$350$ (since, if you win you receive a net profit of (10×36) less 10 dollars, which was your bet), then $(1/37) \times 350 = \$9.46$.

Check: 1 ⊞ 37 ⊠ 350 ⊟   RTR: 9.45945

What is the house's expectancy? If you don't win, the casino receives $10. Hence $(1 - 1/37) = \$9.73$.

Check: 1 ⊞ 37 ⊠ ⊟ 1 ⊞ 1 ⊠ 10 ⊟   RTR: 9.72973

COMPOSED PROBABILITY

Let us consider these four contingencies that can exist between two events:

1. Exclusive
2. Nonexclusive
3. Independent
4. Dependent

1. Two events are *exclusive* if not more than one of them can occur in a single trial. The drawing of a jack and the

drawing of a king at a single drawing are exclusive events: if you draw a jack it is impossible for this card to also be a king.

2. Two events are *nonexclusive* if more than one of them can occur in a single trial. The drawing of a jack and the drawing of a diamond at a single drawing are nonexclusive events: if you draw a jack, it is possible for this card also to be a diamond.

3. Two events are *independent* if the happening of one does not affect the happening of the other. If you throw two dice (or one die twice), the fall of the first die doesn't affect the fall of the second.

4. Two events are *dependent* if the happening of one affects the happening of the other. If you draw two cards from an ordinary deck, the mere fact that you have drawn the first card predetermines that only 51 cards are left in the deck for the second drawing.

Now let's compute the probabilities of such composed events.

1. The probability that one event of a set of exclusive events will happen at a single trial is the sum of the separate probabilities of the events in the set.

$$p_E = p_A + p_B$$

where A and B are exclusive. What is the probability of drawing a queen *or* a jack from an ordinary deck in a single trial? Here the set of exclusive events is the drawing of the queen and the drawing of the jack. Hence $4/52 + 4/52 = 8/52 = 0.\underline{153846}$.

2. The probability that one of a set of nonexclusive events will happen at a single trial is the difference of the sum of the separate probabilities of the events in the set *minus* the product of the same separate probabilities (A and B are nonexclusive events).

$$p_E = (p_A + p_B) - (p_A p_B)$$

Example: What is the probability of drawing a jack or a spade from a deck at a single trial? The probability of drawing a jack is 4/52. The probability of drawing a spade is 13/52 (since there are 13 spades in a deck). Hence: (4/52 + 13/52) − (4/52 × 13/52) = (17/52) − (52/2704) = 0.<u>307692</u>

Check: 17 $\boxed{\div}$ 52 $\boxed{\times}$ 2704 $\boxed{-}$ 52 $\boxed{\div}$ 2704 $\boxed{=}$
RTR: 0.3076922

3. The probability that all the events of a set of independent events will happen in a trial is the product of their separate probabilities (A and B are independent).

$$p_E = p_A p_B$$

Example: Two cards are drawn from an ordinary deck. The first card drawn is replaced at random in the deck before the second card is drawn. What is the probability that both cards are face cards? The two events are independent, since the first card is replaced in the deck before the second drawing. It is equivalent to drawing one card from each of two separate and complete decks. The probability of drawing one face card is 12/52. Hence p_E = 12/52 × 12/52 = (12/52)² = 0.0532544.

4. If the probability that an event will occur is p_A, and if after it has happened the probability that a second and dependent event will occur is p_B, then the probability that the two events will happen in that order is $p_A p_B$ (A and B are dependent).[†]

$$p_E = p_A p_B$$

Example: Two cards are drawn from a deck, as in #3, but here the first card is *not* replaced in the deck. The first event has probability 12/52 = p_A. Now we have only 51 cards left in the deck, and since we presupposed that the first card was already a face card, there are only eleven face cards left. Hence p_B = 11/51. The probability that both A and B are face cards is p_E = (12/52) (11/51) = 0.0497737.

[†] The formulas in 3 and 4 are identical; 4 is a special case of 3.

You will note that the probability is lower when the events are dependent than when they are not.

Before going further, we have to study the computation of the number of ways a set of objects can be arranged. These different arrangements are called *permutation, variation,* and *combination.*

PERMUTATION

The arrangement in all possible manners of the *n* objects of a set taken *all* at the time is a *permutation.*

Example: Arrange the letters *A*, *B*, *C* in all possible manners, using all three letters each time. *n* here is equal to 3.

$$A \ B \ C \qquad B \ A \ C \qquad C \ A \ B$$
$$A \ C \ B \qquad B \ C \ A \qquad C \ B \ A$$

We have six different permutations. Permutation is equal to "factorial n[†]" and is notated:

$$P_n = n!$$

[†] The exclamation point after *n* is read factorial *n*

where: $1! = 1$ $\qquad\qquad 3! = 3 \times 2 \times 1$
$\qquad\;\;\, 2! = 2 \times 1 \qquad\qquad 4! = 4 \times 3 \times 2 \times 1$
$\qquad\qquad\qquad\qquad\qquad\qquad\quad$ etc ....

Thus: $1! = 1 \qquad\qquad\quad 9! = 362880$
$\qquad\;\; 2! = 2 \qquad\qquad\;\, 10! = 3628800$
$\qquad\;\; 3! = 6 \qquad\qquad\;\, 11! = 39916800$
$\qquad\;\; 4! = 24 \qquad\qquad 12! = 479001600$
$\qquad\;\; 5! = 120 \qquad\quad\;\; 13! = 6227020800$
$\qquad\;\; 6! = 720 \qquad\quad\;\; 14! = 87178291200$
$\qquad\;\; 7! = 5040 \qquad\quad\, 15! = 1307674368000$ etc. ...
$\qquad\;\; 8! = 40320 \qquad\;\,$ (70! will be a number composed of 100
$\qquad\qquad\qquad\qquad\qquad\;\;\,$ digits!)

By definition one notes: $0! = 1$

Statistical Operations

You will note that each group of letters in the example is different from the other, and that each group contains all three different letters. They are simply arranged in a different order each time: $P_3 = 3! = 6$. Now, what happens when we want the permutation of n objects among which a objects are of the same sort? That is a permutation of A, A, B.

Permutation of Objects Not All Different

Here

$$_aP_n = \frac{n!}{a!}$$

In our example $n = 3$ and $a = 2$, since we have two objects (A's) of the same sort. Hence

$$_2P_3 = \frac{3!}{2!} = \frac{3 \times 2 \times 1}{2 \times 1} = \frac{3 \times \cancel{2} \times \cancel{1}}{\cancel{2} \times \cancel{1}} = 3$$

Indeed we have

$$AAB$$
$$ABA$$
$$BAA$$

Another example is the permutation of A, A, B, C, C. Here we have two different sorts of objects that are present more than once in the original set (the A's and the C's). To distinguish these two, we put a subscript to a; $a_1 = AA = 2$; $a_2 = CC = 2$; and $n = 5$. The general formula is

$$a_1; a_2; a_3; \ldots ; P_n = \frac{n!}{(a_1!)(a_2!)(\ldots)}$$

To solve our example ($AABCC$) we write:

$$_{2;2}P_5 = \frac{5!}{(2!)(2!)} = \frac{5 \times 4 \times 3 \times 2 \times 1}{(2 \times 1)(2 \times 1)} = 30^\dagger$$

This kind of calculation can be solved with one chain calculation:

5 ☒ 4 ☒ 3 ⊡ 2 ☒ 1 ⊟   RTR: 30

VARIATION

Variation is the arrangement in all possible manners of the n objects of a set taking a limited number k of objects at a time. Variation of n objects taken k at a time is notated:

$$_kV_n$$

Now, unfortunately, we have to complicate things, since there exist two types of variation:

1. The *simple variation* allows each object to be present in each group only once and is notated and solved with:

$$_kV_n = \frac{n!}{(n-k)!}$$

Example: Simple variation of A, B, C in groups of two letters:

$$\begin{array}{cc cc cc} A & B & B & C & C & A \\ B & A & C & B & A & C \end{array}$$

† To simplify such equations, remember that $n!/a! = n(n-1)(n-2)(n-3)\ldots(a+1)$, which means that you have to multiply the numbers from n to $a + 1$ only:

69!/66! = 69 ☒ 68 ☒ 67 ⊟ 314364

Statistical Operations

Here $n = 3$ and $k = 2$. We have six groups. Indeed:

$$_2V_3 = \frac{3!}{(3-2)!} = 3!/1! = 6$$

2. The *complete variation* allows each object to be present in a group up to k times and is notated:

$$_kV_n^* = n^k$$

Example: Complete variation of A, B, C in groups of two letters:

$$\begin{array}{ccc} AA & AB & AC \\ BA & BB & BC \\ CA & CB & CC \end{array}$$

($n = 3$ and $k = 2$). We have nine groups, and indeed:

$$_kV_n^* = {_2V_3^*} = 3^2 = 3 \times 3 = 9$$

This is precisely the computation you need to determine how many different numbers one can produce on a combination lock with three wheels bearing the ten digits (0 to 9) each. The answer is simple: here $n = 10$ and each group will have 3 digits, hence $k = 3$: $_3V_{10}^* = 10^3 = 10 \times 10 \times 10 = 1000$ variations.

Check: 10 ⊠ ⊟ ⊟   RTR: 1000

Thus, if a burglar allows himself 2 seconds per variation to open such a lock, he will succeed in a maximum of 33 minutes and 20 seconds!

Check: 1000 ⊠ 2 ⊞ 60 ⊟   WTR: 33.<u>3</u>

33.<u>3</u> ⊟ 33 ⊠ 60 ⊟   RTR: 19.<u>9</u> = 20

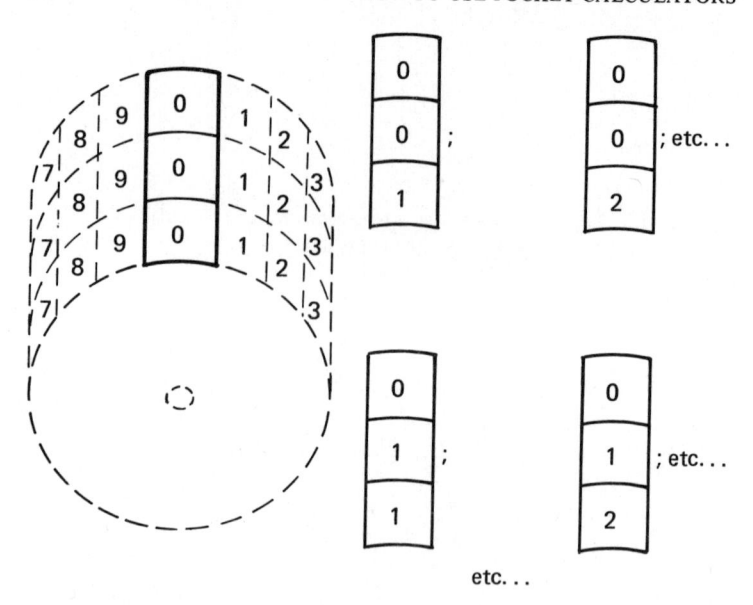

COMBINATION

Combination is the arrangement in all possible manners of the n objects taken k objects at the time *and with regard to their order*.

Here again we have two kinds of combination:

1. The *simple combination* allows each object to be present in each group only once:

$$_kC_n = \frac{n!}{(n-k)!k!}$$

This is also the formula for the binomial coefficients $\binom{n}{k}$.

Example: Combination of A, B, C in groups of 2 letters:

$$A \; B \quad\quad A \; C \quad\quad B \; C$$

where $n = 3$, $k = 2$, and we have three groups!

Statistical Operations

$$_kC_n = {_2C_3} = \frac{3!}{(3-2)!\,2!} = \frac{3 \times 2 \times 1}{1 \times 2 \times 1} = 3$$

2. The *complete combination* allows each object to be present in each group up to k times:

$$_kC_n^* = \frac{(n+k-1)!}{(n-1)!\,k!}$$

Example: Complete combination of A, B, C in groups of 2 letters:

$$
\begin{array}{cc cc cc}
A & A & A & B & A & C \\
  &   & B & B & B & C \\
  &   &   &   & C & C \\
\end{array}
$$

where $n = 3$ and $k = 2$. We have 6 groups:

$$_2C_3^* = \frac{(3+2-1)!}{(3-1)!\,2!} = \frac{4!}{2!\,2!} = \frac{4 \times 3 \times 2 \times 1}{2 \times 1 \times 2 \times 1} = 6$$

Check: 4 ⊠ 3 ⊞ 2 ⊟   RTR: 6

With that knowledge we can return to the study of probabilities in order to solve a problem such as the following: Two dice are tossed six times. What is the probability that 7 will show on exactly four of the tosses? Here we have to know that if p is the probability that an event will happen at a given trial, the probability that it will happen exactly k times in n trials is:

$$p_E = {_kC_n}\,p^k\,(1-p)^{n-k}$$

For this example we write $n = 6$, $k = 4$, and $p = 1/6$. The probability of tossing a 7 *once* is computed as follows: A 7 can be obtained in six ways:

$$
\begin{array}{ll}
\text{1 and 6} & \text{5 and 2} \\
\text{6 and 1} & \text{3 and 4} \\
\text{2 and 5} & \text{4 and 3} \\
\end{array}
$$

Now we have to compute the number of ways two dice may turn up. This is equivalent to computing a complete variation of six objects (digits 1 to 6) in groups of two: $_2V_6^* = 6^2 = 36$ ways.

The probability of a 7 showing up once is therefore $p = 6/36 = 1/6$.

We return to our formula:

$p_E = {_kC_n} p^k (1 - p)^{n-k}$

$p_E = {_4C_6} (1/6)^4 (1 - 1/6)^{6-4}$

$p_E = \left(\dfrac{6!}{(6-4)!\, 4!} \right) (1/6)^4 (1 - 1/6)^2$

$p_E = \left(\dfrac{6 \times 5 \times 4 \times 3 \times 2 \times 1}{2 \times 1 \times 4 3 \times 2 \times 1} \right) (1/6)^4 (5/6)^2$

$p_E = (30/2)(1/6)(1/6)(1/6)(1/6)(5/6)(5/6)$

$p_E = 5 \;\boxed{\times}\; 30 \;\boxed{=}\;\boxed{=}\;\boxed{+}\; 2 \;\boxed{\div}\; 6 \;\boxed{=}\;\boxed{=}\;\boxed{=}\;\boxed{=}\;\boxed{=}\;\boxed{=}$

$p_E = 0.0080375$

This is rather low, isn't it? It's equivalent to about eight successes in 1,000 trials. Remember that *one* success is having 7 turn up four times when two dice are tossed six times; *one* trial being the *six* tosses.

PART FIVE

SCIENTIFIC (EXPONENTIAL) NOTATION

CHAPTER 14

DESCRIPTION OF SCIENTIFIC NOTATION

In the chapter related to special constants it would mean exactly the same thing to write that c (the speed of light in vacuum) is equal to 299792500 m/s, or to say that the gravitational constant is equal to 0.00000000006670 Newton m^2/kg^2 as opposed to:

$c = 2.997925 \cdot 10^8 \text{ m s}^{-1}$ and $G = 6.670 \cdot 10^{-11}$ Newton $m^2 \text{ kg}^{-2}$.

It is, however, easier to work with the latter notation once you have gotten used to it, since you don't have to stop to count the number of zeros or figures before or after the decimal point. Another obvious advantage is that with this notation you can work with very large numbers or very small fractions on your eight-digit calculator.

If you wanted to write 10 million in the traditional fashion, you would write 10,000,000. This number can also be expressed by the following multiplications: $10 \times 10 \times 10 \times 10 \times 10 \times 10 \times 10 = 10,000,000$. You recognize these multiplications as being 10 raised to its 7th power. (Seven 10's multiplied together): $10^7 = 10,000,000$.

By the same principle, the distance to a galaxy can be expressed as 10^{18} miles, which is much more economical than 1,000,000,000,000,000,000 miles (there are no less than 18 zeros in this number). We know then that 10^2 is equal to $10 \times 10 = 100$ (two zeros); 10^3 is equal to $10 \times 10 \times 10 = 1000$ (three zeros); 10^4 is equal to 10,000 (four zeros); and so on. 7.5×10^2 (also notated $7.5 \cdot 10^2$) is then equal to $7.5 \times 100 = 750$. Thus $7.5 \cdot 10^2$ is the scientific notation for the traditional 750! Another example is $3.4 \cdot 10^6$, which is equal to $3.4 \times 1,000,000 = 3,400,000$.

Note: As a rule, the number that is multiplied by the proper power of 10 is chosen as to be between 1 and 10.

Example: Write 54,670,000 in scientific notation. The number between 1 and 10 will then be 5.467 (these are the *significant digits*). We want to multiply 5.467 by the proper power of ten. In this case, we want to multiply it by 10,000,000. Since 10,000,000 has seven zeros, we can write $10,000,000 = 10^7$. Thus, $54,670,000 = 5.467 \cdot 10^7$.

If we wanted to translate $5.467 \cdot 10^7$ in the traditional notation, we would simply shift the decimal point after 5 *seven places to the right*—5 4/6/7/ / / / /—and fill the spaces with zeros: 5 4/6/7/0/0/0/0/. Thus we have: 54,670,000.

To translate $7.534 \cdot 10^9$ we write (7 5/3/4/0/0/0/0/0/); thus, 7,534,000,000.

This counting method can also be used to translate *into* scientific notation. To translate 654,800,000,000 we count from *right to left* until we have shifted the decimal point *just before the last digit* in order to get the number between 1 and 10: 6/5/4/8/0/0/0/0/0/0/0 = eleven places; thus, 654,800,000,000 = $6.548 \cdot 10^{11}$.

To translate 87,642,070,000 we write (8/7/6/4/2/0/7/0/0/0/) = ten places; thus, $87,642,070,000 = 8.764207 \cdot 10^{10}$.

So far we have demonstrated the scientific notation of large numbers. Small fractions can also be expressed in this handy notation. You will remember that a number N raised to a *negative power* $-P$ is equal to the reciprocal of the number N raised to the positive power P. Examples:

Scientific Exponential Notation

$$2^{-2} \text{ is equal to } \frac{1}{2^2} = 1/4 = 0.25$$

Check: 2 ⊠ ⊟ ⊞ ⊟ ⊟   RTR: 0.25

$$5^{-3} = \frac{1}{5 \times 5 \times 5} = 1/125 = 0.008$$

Check: 5 ⊠ ⊟ ⊟ ⊞ ⊟ ⊟   RTR: 0.008

$$10^{-4} = \frac{1}{10 \times 10 \times 10 \times 10} = 1/10000 = 0.0001$$

Check: 10 ⊠ ⊟ ⊟ ⊟ ⊞ ⊟ ⊟   RTR: 0.0001

In this last example you will note that in 0.0001 we have four zeros if we include in the count the zero on the left of the decimal point. We know then that 10^{-2} is equal to $1/100 = 0.01$ (two zeros); 10^{-3} is equal to $1/1000 = 0.001$ (three zeros); 10^{-4} is equal to $1/10000 = 0.0001$ (four zeros); and so on. Thus, 7.5×10^{-2} (also notated $7.5 \cdot 10^{-2}$) is equal to $7.5 \times 0.01 = 0.075$. $7.5 \cdot 10^{-2}$ is the scientific notation for the traditional 0.075 and $3.4 \cdot 10^{-6}$ is equal to $3.4 \times 1/1000000 = 3.4 \times 0.000001 = 0.0000034$.

Example: Write 0.000000314 in scientific notation. The number between 1 and 10 is here 3.14 (again called the significant digits). We want to multiply 3.14 by the proper power of ten. In this case, we want to multiply it by 0.0000001. Since 0.0000001 has seven zeros (including the zero on the left of the decimal point), we can write $0.0000001 = 10^{-7}$, and thus $0.000000314 = 3.14 \cdot 10^{-7}$.

If we wanted to translate $3.14 \cdot 10^{-7}$ in the traditional notation, we would simply shift the decimal point after 3 *seven places to the left*—/ / / / / / /3 14—and fill the spaces with zeros: 0/0/0/0/0/0/0/3 14. We have 0.000000314.

Example: Translate $7.534 \cdot 10^{-9}$. We write (/ / / / / / / / /7 534); thus 0.000000007534.

Here, too, this counting method can also be used to translate *into* scientific notation. To translate 0.0000627 we count *from left to right* until we have shifted the decimal point just after the first significant digit in order to get the "number between 1 and 10": $0\,0/0/0/0/6/27$ = five places; thus, $0.0000627 = 6.27 \cdot 10^{-5}$.

To translate 0.000006507 we write $(0\,0/0/0/0/0/6/507)$ = six places; thus, $0.000006507 = 6.507 \cdot 10^{-6}$.

CHAPTER 15

THE OPERATIONS

We can use this scientific notation to operate on very large (or very small) numbers with our eight-digit pocket calculators.

RULE: When two numbers (scientifically notated) are multiplied, between them, their significant digits are multiplied and *their exponents (of ten) are added.* The exponent of the result is then corrected in order to have a significant number between 1 and 10.

Example: $(3.76 \cdot 10^4) \times (7.08 \cdot 10^2)$. First multiply the significant digits $3.76 \times 7.08 = 26.6208$. Then add the two exponents $4 + 2 = 6$. The rough result is $26.6208 \cdot 10^6$. Since the significant number (26.6208) is larger than 10, we correct the answer by shifting the decimal point to the left *one place and adding 1* to the exponent of 10. The final result is thus $2.66208 \cdot 10^7$.

Since these numbers are not too large, let's check this with our calculator: $3.76 \cdot 10^4$ is equal to 37,600; $7.08 \cdot 10^2$ is equal to 708.

Compute: 37600 ⊠ 708 = WTR: 26,620,800

And indeed 26,620,800 is equal to $2.66208 \cdot 10^7$.

Let's stop a minute to explain how the final correction was made. As we have seen, 26.6208 was larger than 10. To bring this number to its proper magnitude (between 1 and 10) we shifted its decimal point *one* place to the left. This was equivalent to dividing 26.6208 by 10. Since we divided the significant number by 10, we had to multiply the rest of the result by 10 in order to get the proper answer: $10^6 \times 10$ is equal to 10^7. Check: $10^6 = 10 \times 10 \times 10 \times 10 \times 10 \times 10$. If we multiply this by ten we have $(10 \times 10 \times 10 \times 10 \times 10 \times 10) \times 10$. We remove the parentheses and we have $10 \times 10 \times 10 \times 10 \times 10 \times 10 \times 10$. In other words seven 10's multiplied together, which is equivalent to 10^7.

Another example is $(8.08 \cdot 10^{34}) \times (9 \cdot 10^1)$. Here we multiply the significant digits—$8.08 \times 9 = 72.72$—add the two exponents—$34 + 1 = 35$—and get a rough result of $72.72 \cdot 10^{35}$. Correction: $7.272 \cdot 10^{36}$, which is our final answer.

RULE: When one number is the divisor of another number (both scientifically notated), the significant digits of the latter are *divided* by the significant digits of the first and the exponent of the first is *subtracted* from the exponent of the second. The exponent of the result is then corrected (when necessary) in order to have a significant number between 1 and 10.

Example: $\dfrac{6.75 \cdot 10^4}{8.5 \cdot 10^3}.$

We first divide the first significant digits by those of the second number: $6.75 \div 8.5 = 0.7941176$. Then subtract the second exponent from the first: $4 - 3 = 1$. The rough answer is $0.7941176 \cdot 10^1$. This is corrected as follows: Since 0.7941176 is less than 1, we multiply it by 10 by shifting the decimal point one place to the right and subtracting 1 from the exponent: $0.7941176 \cdot 10^1$ becomes $7.941176 \cdot 10^0$. Since by definition $10^0 = 1$, we have $7.941176 \cdot 1 = 7.941176$, which is our final answer.

Check: $6.75 \cdot 10^4$ is equivalent to $67{,}500$
$8.5 \cdot 10^3$ is equivalent to $8{,}500$

Scientific Exponential Notation 135

Compute: 67500 $\boxed{\div}$ 8500 = RTR: 7.9411764

Another example is $\dfrac{6.645 \cdot 10^{32}}{7.934 \cdot 10^{65}}$.

Division with the significant digits yields 6.645 ÷ 7.934 = 0.8375346. Then subtraction with the exponents, 32 − 65 = − 33, gives the rough result $0.8375346 \cdot 10^{-33}$. And the correction: $8.375346 \cdot 10^{-34}$. (Here we multiplied the significant digits by 10 and thus subtracted one from the exponent: − 33 − 1 = − 34.)

RULE: To add or subtract two scientifically notated numbers, convert the smaller number's exponent (and therefore its significant digits) to have an identical exponent for both numbers. The two numbers are then added or subtracted. The exponent of the result (rough) will be the same as of those of the terms. The result is then corrected when necessary in order to have a significant number between 1 and 10.

Example: $(4.7 \cdot 10^5) + (6.2 \cdot 10^4)$. We first change the second term of the addition in order to get 5 as an exponent (which is the exponent of the largest term): $6.2 \cdot 10^4$ is equivalent to $0.62 \cdot 10^5$. Here we added 1 to the exponent and thus divided the significant digits by 10. We can now perform the addition, 4.7 + 0.62 = 5.32, and get the result $5.32 \cdot 10^5$. This is acceptable since the significant number is already between 1 and 10.

Another example is $(9.6 \cdot 10^8) - (6.234 \cdot 10^6)$. Conversion of the smaller term $(6.234 \cdot 10^6)$ is equivalent to $0.06234 \cdot 10^8$. We compute 9.6 − 0.06234 = 9.53766 and get the result $9.53766 \cdot 10^8$, which doesn't need correction.

Another example is $(8.66 \cdot 10^{67}) + (6.88 \cdot 10^{67})$. Here there is no need of converting either term since both have the same exponent. We compute—8.66 + 6.88 = 15.54—and get the rough result $15.54 \cdot 10^{67}$. The correction is $1.554 \cdot 10^{68}$.

Here is a little trick that might help you in converting or correcting such scientifically notated numbers: When the decimal point comes *closer* to the exponent, this one gets *smaller*.

When the decimal point moves *away* from the exponent, this one gets *larger*. I'm sure that the reader will be able to construct a psychological analogy without any difficulty in order to remember this helpful technique!

Table 15.1

Name (U.S. & French Systems)	Scientific Notation	Traditional Notation	Metric Prefixes
One quintillionth	$1 \cdot 10^{-18}$ =	0.000000000000000001	atto (a)
One quadrillionth	$1 \cdot 10^{-15}$ =	0.000000000000001	femto (f)
One trillionth	$1 \cdot 10^{-12}$ =	0.000000000001	pico (p)
One billionth	$1 \cdot 10^{-9}$ =	0.000000001	nano (n)
One millionth	$1 \cdot 10^{-6}$ =	0.000001	micro (μ)
One thousandth	$1 \cdot 10^{-3}$ =	0.001	milli (m)
One hundredth	$1 \cdot 10^{-2}$ =	0.01	centi (c)
One tenth	$1 \cdot 10^{-1}$ =	0.1	deci (d)
One	$1 \cdot 10^{0}$ =	1	*unity*
Ten	$1 \cdot 10^{1}$ =	10	deca (da)
One hundred	$1 \cdot 10^{2}$ =	100	hecto (h)
One thousand	$1 \cdot 10^{3}$ =	1000	kilo (k)
One million	$1 \cdot 10^{6}$ =	1,000,000	mega (M)
One billion	$1 \cdot 10^{9}$ =	1,000,000,000	giga (G)
One trillion	$1 \cdot 10^{12}$ =	1,000,000,000,000	tera (T)
One quadrillion	$1 \cdot 10^{15}$ =	1,000,000,000,000,000	
One quintillion	$1 \cdot 10^{18}$	etc...	
One sextillion	$1 \cdot 10^{21}$		
One septillion	$1 \cdot 10^{24}$		
One octillion	$1 \cdot 10^{27}$		
One nonillion	$1 \cdot 10^{30}$		
One decillion	$1 \cdot 10^{33}$		
One undecillion	$1 \cdot 10^{36}$		
One duodecillion	$1 \cdot 10^{39}$		

APPENDIX A

VARIOUS TABLES, FORMULAS, AND SYMBOLS

This section offers the ambitious reader a few useful formulas, tables, and constant values related to mathematics a bit more complicated than we have so far seen.

SPECIAL CONSTANTS

π = 3.14159 26535 89793 23846 26433 83279 50288 41971 69399 37510...

$\pi \simeq \frac{355}{113} = 3.14159 2920...$

1 radian = $180°/\pi$ = 57.29577 95130 823...°

1° = $\pi/180°$ = 0.01745 32925 19943 29576 92... radian

e = 2.71828 18284 59045 23536... = $\lim_{n\to\infty}(1 + 1/n)^n \simeq \frac{1264}{465}$

e = natural base of logarithms

$\log_e 10 = \ln 10$ = 2.30258 50929 94045 68401 7991... $\simeq \frac{624}{271}$

137

$c = 2.997925 \cdot 10^8 \ m \cdot s^{-1}$ = Speed of light in vacuum

$G = 6.670 \cdot 10^{-11}$ Newton$\cdot m^2 \cdot kg^{-2}$ = Gravitational constant

Light-year = $9.46 \cdot 10^{12} \ km$ = $5.9 \cdot 10^{12}$ miles

Table A.1
Special Formulas

Formulas	Examples
$A + B = B + A$	$5 + 3 = 3 + 5 = 8$
$AB = BA$	$5 \cdot 3 = 3 \cdot 5 = 15$
$A(B + C) = AB + AC$	$3(5 + 7) = (3 \cdot 5) + (3 \cdot 7) = 15 + 21 = 36$
$(A + B)C = AC + BC$	$(3 + 5)7 = (3 \cdot 7) + (5 \cdot 7) = 21 + 35 = 56$
$A + (B + C) = (A + B) + C$	$3 + (5 + 7) = (3 + 5) + 7 = 15$
$A(BC) = (AB)C$	$3(5 \cdot 7) = (3 \cdot 5)7 = 105$
If $AB = 0$, then $A = 0$ or $B = 0$	$8 \times 0 = 0; \ 0 \times 8 = 0$
$A + (+B) = A + B$	$3 + (+5) = 3 + 5 = 8$
$A + (-B) = A - B$	$3 + (-5) = 3 - 5 = -2$
$A - (+B) = A - B$	$3 - (+5) = 3 - 5 = -2$
$A - (-B) = A + B$	$3 - (-5) = 3 + 5 = 8$
$(+A)(+B) = +AB$	$(+3)(+5) = +(3 \cdot 5) = 15$
$(+A)(-B) = -AB$	$(+3)(-5) = -(3 \cdot 5) = -15$
$(-A)(+B) = -AB$	$(-3)(+5) = -(3 \cdot 5) = -15$
$(-A)(-B) = +AB$	$(-3)(-5) = +(3 \cdot 5) = 15$
$+A/+B = +(A/B)$	$+3/+5 = +(3/5) = 0.6$
$+A/-B = -(A/B)$	$+3/-5 = -(3/5) = -0.6$
$-A/+B = -(A/B)$	$-3/+5 = -(3/5) = -0.6$
$-A/-B = +(A/B)$	$-3/-5 = +(3/5) = 0.6$
$A^n = AA \cdots A$ (n times)	$3^5 = 3 \cdot 3 \cdot 3 \cdot 3 \cdot 3 = 243$
$A^{-n} = 1/A^n$	$3^{-5} = 1/3^5 = 1/243 = 0.0041152$
$A^m A^n = A^{m+n}$	$3^5 \cdot 3^7 = 3^{5+7} = 3^{12} = 531441$
$A^m/A^n \ A^{m-n}$	$3^5/3^7 = 3^{5-7} = 3^{-2} = 0.\underline{1}$
$(A^m)^n = A^{mn}$	$(3^5)^7 = 3^{5 \cdot 7} = 3^{35} = 5.003154592 \cdot 10^{16}$

Various Tables, Formulas, and Symbols

Formulas

$A^0 = 1$
$A^1 = A$
$1/A^{-n} = A^n$
$(AB)^n = A^n B^n$

$(A/B)^n = A^n/B^n$

$(A^m)^{-n} = 1/A^{mn}$

$\sqrt[n]{A} = A^{1/n}$
If $A > 1$, then $\sqrt[\infty]{A} = \infty$
$\sqrt[1]{A} = A$
$\sqrt[-n]{A} = 1/\sqrt[n]{A}$
$\sqrt[m]{A} \sqrt[n]{A} = A^{(n+m)/mn}$

$\sqrt[m]{A}/\sqrt[n]{A} = A^{(n-m)/mn}$

$\sqrt[n]{A^m} = A^{m/n}$
$1/\sqrt[n]{A} = \sqrt[n]{A}$
$\sqrt[n]{AB} = \sqrt[n]{A} / \sqrt[n]{B}$

$\sqrt[n]{A/B} = \sqrt[n]{A} / \sqrt[n]{B}$

$\sqrt[-n]{A^m} = 1/A^{m/n}$

If
$ax^2 + bx + c = 0$, then
$$x_1 = \frac{-b + \sqrt{b^2 - 4ac}}{2a} \quad \text{and}$$

$$x_2 = \frac{-b - \sqrt{b^2 - 4ac}}{2a}$$

where if a, b, c are real numbers,

Examples

$10^0 = 1$
$10^1 = 10$
$1/3^{-5} = 3^5 = 243$
$(3 \cdot 5)^7 = 3^7 \cdot 5^7 = 15^7 =$
  $2187 \cdot 78125 = 170859375$

$(3/5)^7 = 3^7/5^7 = 0.6^7 =$
  $2187/78125 = 0.0279936$

$(3^5)^{-7} = 1/3^{5 \cdot 7} = 1/3^{35}$
  $= 1.998738959 \cdot 10^{-17}$

$\sqrt[3]{8} = 8^{1/3} = 8^{0.3} = 2$
$\sqrt[\infty]{8} = \infty$
$\sqrt[1]{8} = 8$
$\sqrt[-3]{8} = 1/\sqrt[3]{8} = 1/2 = 0.5$
$\sqrt[3]{64} \cdot \sqrt[2]{64} = 64^{(2+3)/2 \cdot 3} = 64^{5/6}$
  $= 64^{0.8\overline{3}} = 32$
$\sqrt[3]{64} / \sqrt[2]{64} = 64^{(2-3)/2 \cdot 3} = 64^{-1/6}$
  $= 64^{-0.1\overline{6}} = 0.5$
$\sqrt[2]{64^3} = 64^{3/2} = 64^{1.5} = 512$
$1/\sqrt[3]{64} = \sqrt[3]{64} = 4$
$\sqrt[3]{(16)(4)} = \sqrt[3]{16} \cdot \sqrt[3]{4} =$
  $2.5198 \ldots \times 1.5874 \ldots = 4$
$\sqrt[3]{(16/2)} = \sqrt[3]{16}/\sqrt[3]{2} =$
  $2.5198 \ldots / 1.2599 \ldots = 2$
$\sqrt[-3]{2^5} = 1/2^{5/3} = 1/2^{1.6_-} =$
  $0.314980262 \ldots$

$2x^2 - 7x + 3 = 0$
$$x_1 = \frac{+7 + \sqrt{7^2 - (4)(2)(3)}}{(2)(2)}$$
$$= \frac{7 + \sqrt{25}}{4} = \frac{12}{4} = 3$$
$$x_2 = \frac{+7 - \sqrt{7^2 - (4)(2)(3)}5}{(2)(2)}$$
$$= \frac{7 - \sqrt{25}}{4} = \frac{2}{4} = \frac{1}{2}$$

and if $b^2 - 4ac > 0$, then the roots (x_1 and x_2) are real and unequal;
$b^2 - 4ac < 0$, then the roots are imaginary and unequal;
$b^2 - 4ac = 0$, then the roots are real and equal.

SPECIAL PRODUCTS AND FACTORS

$x^2 - y^2 = (x + y)(x - y)$

$x^3 + y^3 = (x + y)(x^2 - xy + y^2)$

$x^3 - y^3 = (x - y)(x^2 + xy + y^2)$

$x^4 - y^4 = (x + y)(x - y)(x^2 + y^2)$

$x^5 + y^5 = (x + y)(x^4 - x^3y + x^2y^2 - xy^3 + y^4)$

$x^5 - y^5 = (x - y)(x^4 + x^3y + x^2y^2 + xy^3 + y^4)$

$\dfrac{a^n - b^n}{a - b} = a^{n-1} + a^{n-2}b + a^{n-3}b^2 + \ldots + ab^{n-2} + b^{n-1}$

where n is a positive integer

$\dfrac{a^n + b^n}{a + b} = a^{n-1} - a^{n-2}b + a^{n-3}b^2 - \ldots + (-1)^{n-2}ab^{n-2} + (-1)^{n-1}b^{n-1}$

where n is an odd positive integer

$(x \pm y)^2 = x^2 \pm 2xy + y^2$

$(x \pm y)^3 = x^3 \pm 3x^2y + 3xy^2 \pm y^3$

$(x \pm y)^4 = x^4 \pm 4x^3y + 6x^2y^2 \pm 4xy^3 + y^4$

The results above are special cases of the Binomial Formula:

Binomial Formula for Positive Integer n:

If $n = 1, 2, 3, \ldots$ then

$(x + y)^n = (_0C_n)x^{n-0}y^0 + (_1C_n)x^{n-1}y^1 + (_2C_n)x^{n-2}y^2 + \ldots$
$\qquad + (_nC_n)x^0y^n$

Remember that $_kC_n = \dfrac{n!}{k!(n-k)!}$ (see page 124).

Various Tables, Formulas, and Symbols

THE GREEK ALPHABET

A	α	alpha	N	ν	nu
B	β	beta	Ξ	ξ	xi
Γ	γ	gamma	O	o	omicron
Δ	δ	delta	Π	π	pi
E	ε	epsilon	P	ρ	rho
Z	ζ	zeta	Σ	σ	sigma
H	η	eta	T	τ	tau
Θ	θ	theta	Υ	υ	upsilon
I	ι	iota	Φ	φ	phi
K	κ	kappa	X	χ	chi
Λ	λ	lambda	Ψ	ψ	psi
M	μ	mu	Ω	ω	omega

OTHER SYMBOLS

$\sqrt{}$	= Radical sign	π	=	pi = 3.14159...
{ }	= Braces	<	=	less than
±	= Plus or minus	>	=	greater than
Σ	= The sum of	·	=	"times" as "×"
∫	= Integral	≃	=	Approximately equal to
[ ]	= Brackets			
( )	= Parentheses	∞	=	Infinity
Δ	= Change / Increment	...	=	And so on / Etc.
→	= Towards	$\lim_{x \to \infty}$	=	As "x" approaches infinity as a limit
Π	= The product of			
		!	=	Factorial
		%	=	Percent / Per hundred

APPENDIX B

SERIES

ARITHMETIC SERIES

$a_1 + (a_1 + d) + (a_1 + 2d) + \ldots + a_k + \ldots + a_n$
where: a_1 = First term
d = Difference of two successive terms (constant)
a_k = Term of kth rank
a_n = Last term
n = Number of terms
S = Sum of the series

Then: $a_k = a_1 + (k - 1)d \quad S = \left(\dfrac{a_1 + a_n}{2}\right)n = \dfrac{n}{2}\left[2a_1 + (n - 1)d\right]$
$a_n = a_1 + (n - 1)d$
$n = \dfrac{a_n - a_1}{d} + 1$

Example: Consider the following series

$$1 + 3 + 5 + \ldots + 29$$

Here $a_1 = 1$ and $a_n = 29$ and $d = 2$
The 10th term will then be: $1 + (10 - 1)2$
Compute: 10 ⊟ 1 ⊠ 2 ⊞ 1 ⊟   RTR: 19
There is $\dfrac{29 - 1}{2} + 1 = 15$ terms in the series

143

Check: 29 ⊟ 1 ⊞ 2 ⊞ 1 ⊟   RTR: 15

The sum is: $\left(\dfrac{1+29}{2}\right) 15 = 225$ or $\dfrac{15}{2}[2 \cdot 1 + (15-1)2] = 225$

Check: 29 ⊞ 1 ⊟ 2 ⊠ 15 ⊟ or 15 ⊟ 1 ⊠ 2 ⊞ 2 ⊠ 15 ⊞ 2 ⊟   RTR: 225

GEOMETRIC SERIES

$a_1 + a_1 r + a_1 r^2 + a_1 r^3 + \ldots + a_k + \ldots + a_n$

where: a_1 = first term
r = ratio of two successive terms (constant)
a_k = term of kth rank
a_n = last term
n = number of terms
S_n = Sum of the series

Then: $a_k = a_1 r^{k-1}$

$a_n = a_1 r^{n-1}$

The geometric series is divergent for $r > 1$, convergent for $0 < r < 1$, alternating for $r < 0$, and is a series of n constant terms for $r = 1$, in which case $S_n = na_1$

If $r > 1$ and $n < \infty$

$$S_n = \dfrac{a_n r - a_1}{r - 1} = \dfrac{a_1(r^n - 1)}{r - 1}$$

If $r < 1$ and $n < \infty$

$$S_n = \dfrac{a_1 - a_n r}{1 - r} = \dfrac{a_1(1 - r^n)}{r}$$

If $-1 < r < 1$ and $n = \infty$ (*Infinite* series)

$$S_\infty = \dfrac{a_1}{1-r}$$

Example: $3 - 3/2 + 3/4 - 3/8 + 3/16 - \ldots$ Here $r = -1/2$

$$S_\infty = \dfrac{3}{1 + 1/2} = 2$$

Check: 1 ⊞ 2 ⊞ 1 ⊞ ⊟ ⊟ ⊠ 3 ⊟   RTR: 1.9̄ = 2

APPENDIX C

GEOMETRIC FORMULAS

Generalized Steps are given whenever a single chain calculation is possible.

PLANE GEOMETRY

Square

$Area = s^2$
s ⊠ ⊟   RTR: Area
$Perimeter = 4s$
4 ⊠ s ⊟   RTR: Perimeter
$Diagonal = s\sqrt{2}$
1.4142136 ⊠ s ⊟   RTR: Diagonal

Rectangle

$Area = ab$
a ⊠ b ⊟   RTR: Area
$Perimeter = 2a + 2b$
a ⊞ b ⊠ 2 ⊟   RTR: Perimeter
$Diagonal = \sqrt{a^2 + b^2}$

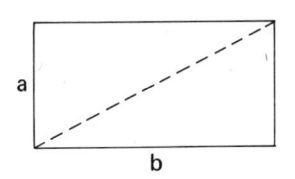

145

Parallelogram

$Area = ab = bc \sin \theta$
$a \boxtimes b \boxminus$ RTR: Area
$b \boxtimes c \boxtimes \sin \theta \boxminus$ RTR: Area
$Perimeter = 2b + 2c$
$b \boxplus c \boxtimes 2 \boxminus$ RTR: Perimeter

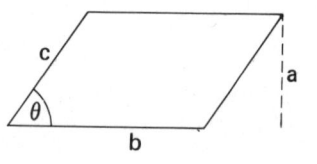

Triangle

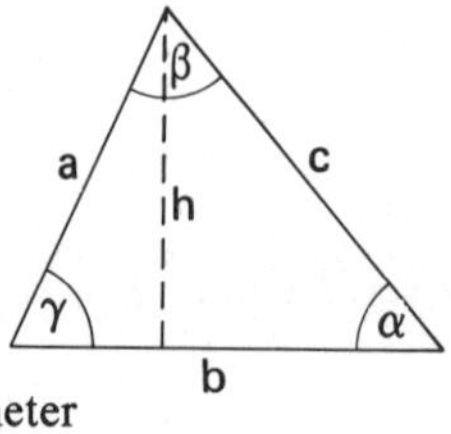

$Perimeter = a + b + c$
$a \boxplus b \boxplus c \boxminus$ RTR: Perimeter
$Semiperimeter = \dfrac{a+b+c}{2} = S$
$a \boxplus b \boxplus c \boxplus 2 \boxminus$ RTR: Semiperimeter
$Area = \dfrac{bh}{2} = \dfrac{ab \sin \gamma}{2} = \sqrt{S(S-a)(S-b)(S-c)}$
$= \dfrac{a^2 \sin \beta \sin \gamma}{2 \sin \alpha}$
$b \boxtimes h \boxplus 2 \boxminus$ RTR: Area
$a \boxtimes b \boxtimes \sin \gamma \boxminus$ RTR: Area
$a \boxtimes \boxminus \boxtimes \sin \beta \boxtimes \sin \gamma \boxplus 2 \boxplus \sin \alpha \boxminus$ RTR: Area

Right Triangle

$Hypotenuse = \sqrt{a^2 + b^2}$
$Area = \dfrac{ab}{2}$
$a \boxtimes b \boxplus 2 \boxminus$ RTR: Area

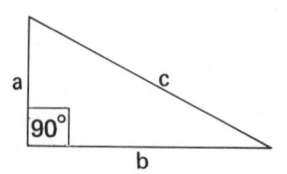

Equilateral Triangle

$Area = \dfrac{a^2 \sqrt{3}}{4}$
$a \boxtimes \boxminus \boxtimes 0.43301270 \boxminus$ RTR: Area

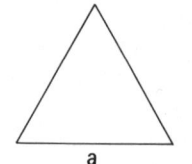

Geometric Formulas

Trapezoid

$Area = \dfrac{h(a+b)}{2}$

a ⊞ b ⊠ h ⊞ 2 ⊟   RTR: Area

$Perimeter = a + b + h(1/\sin\alpha + 1/\sin\beta) = a + b + h(\csc\alpha + \csc\beta)$

$\sin\alpha$ ⊞ $\sin\beta$ ⊞ $\sin\alpha$ ⊞ $\sin\beta$ ⊠ h ⊞ a ⊞ b ⊟   RTR: Perimeter

$\csc\alpha$ ⊞ $\csc\beta$ ⊠ h ⊞ a ⊞ b ⊟   RTR: Perimeter

Regular Polygon of *n* Sides

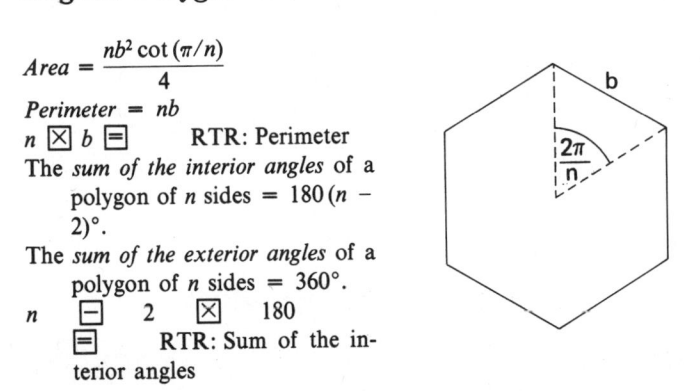

$Area = \dfrac{nb^2 \cot(\pi/n)}{4}$

$Perimeter = nb$

n ⊠ b ⊟   RTR: Perimeter

The *sum of the interior angles* of a polygon of *n* sides = $180(n-2)°$.

The *sum of the exterior angles* of a polygon of *n* sides = $360°$.

n ⊟ 2 ⊠ 180 ⊟   RTR: Sum of the interior angles

Circle

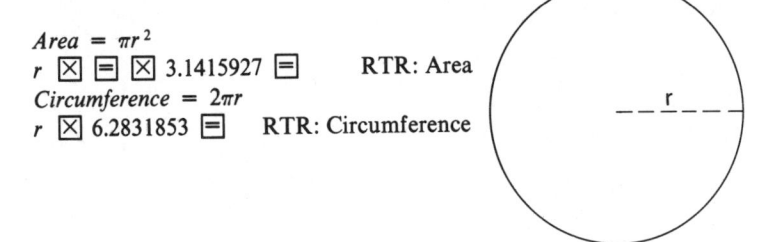

$Area = \pi r^2$

r ⊠ ⊟ ⊠ 3.1415927 ⊟   RTR: Area

$Circumference = 2\pi r$

r ⊠ 6.2831853 ⊟   RTR: Circumference

Sector of Circle

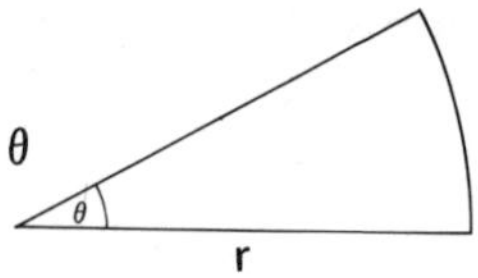

(θ in radians)
Area = $\frac{1}{2}(r^2\theta)$
r ☒ ▭ ☒ θ ⊞ 2 ▭   RTR: Area
Arc length = $r\theta$
r ☒ θ ▭   RTR: Arc length
If the angle is in degrees, then:
r ☒ $\theta°$ ⊞ 57.295780 ▭   RTR: Arc length

Segment of Circle

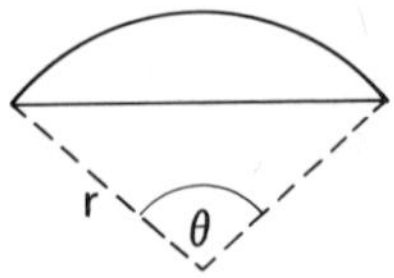

(θ in radians)
Area = $\frac{1}{2}r^2(\theta - \sin\theta)$
θ ⊟ sin θ ☒ r ☒ r ⊞ 2 ▭   RTR: Area
If the angle is in degrees, then:
Area = $(\theta°/360)(\pi r^2) - \frac{1}{2}r^2 \sin\theta°$
0.01745329 ☒ $\theta°$ ⊟ sin $\theta°$ ☒ r ☒ r ⊞ 2
▭   RTR: Area

Ellipse

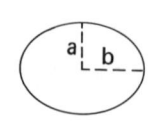

Area = $ab\pi$
π ☒ a ☒ b ▭   RTR: Area
Perimeter = $4a \int_0^{\pi/2} \sqrt{1 - (\sqrt{a^2 - b^2}/a)^2 \sin^2\theta}\, d\theta$
$\simeq 2\pi\sqrt{\frac{1}{2}(a^2 + b^2)}$

SOLID GEOMETRY

Rectangular Parallelepiped

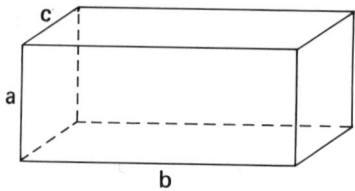

Volume = abc
a ☒ b ☒ c ▭   RTR: Volume
Surface area = $2(ab + ac + bc)$

Parallelepiped

$Volume = ach = abc \sin \theta$
$a \boxtimes c \boxtimes h \boxminus$ RTR: Volume
$a \boxtimes b \boxtimes c \boxtimes \sin \theta \boxminus$
  RTR: Volume

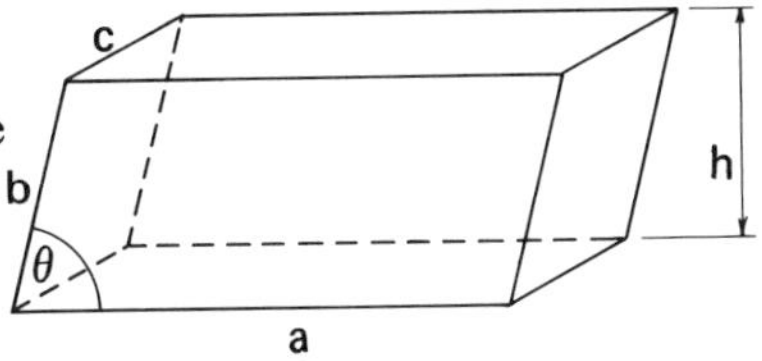

Pyramid

$Volume = \dfrac{Bh}{3}$
Base surface $\boxtimes h \boxplus 3 \boxminus$ RTR: Volume

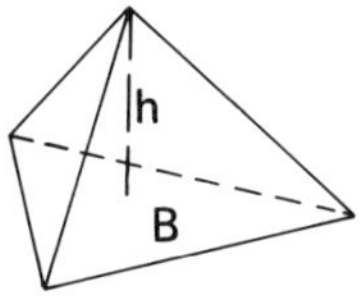

Right Circular Cone or Cone of Revolution

$Volume = \dfrac{\pi r^2 h}{3}$
$r \boxtimes \boxminus \boxtimes 1.0471976 \boxtimes h \boxminus$ RTR: Volume
$Lateral\ surface\ area = \pi r \sqrt{r^2 + h^2} = \pi r L$
$3.1415927 \boxtimes r \boxtimes L \boxminus$ Lateral surface area
$Total\ area = \pi r (L + r)$

$L \boxplus r \boxtimes r \boxtimes 3.1415927 \boxminus$ RTR: Total area

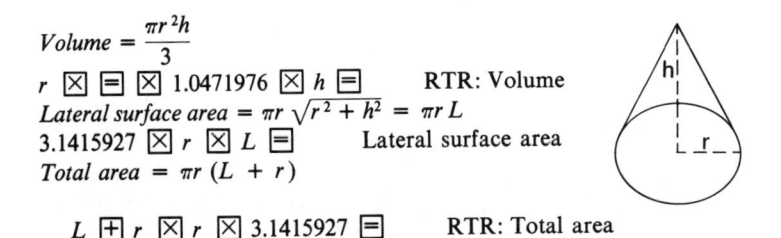

Sphere

$Volume = \dfrac{\pi 4 r^3}{3}$
$r \boxtimes \boxminus \boxminus \boxtimes 4.1887902 \boxminus$ RTR: Volume

$Surface\ area = 4\pi r^2$

$r \boxtimes \boxminus \boxtimes 12.566371 \boxminus$ RTR: Surface area

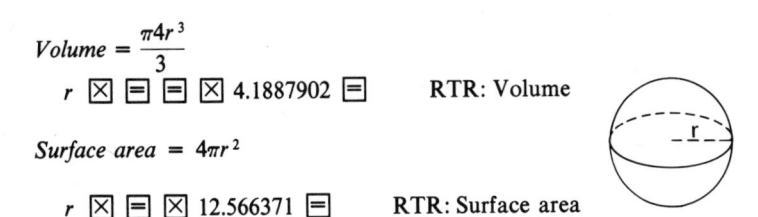

Right Circular Cylinder or Cylinder of Revolution

Volume $= \pi r^2 h$

r ☒ ☐ ☒ 3.1415927 ☒ h ☐   RTR: Volume

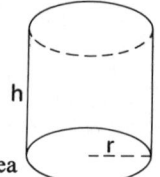

Lateral surface area $= 2\pi r h$

r ☒ h ☒ 6.2831853 ☐   RTR: Lateral surface area

Total area $= 2\pi r (h + r)$

h ⊞ r ☒ r ☒ 6.2831853 ☐   RTR: Total area

Circular Cylinder

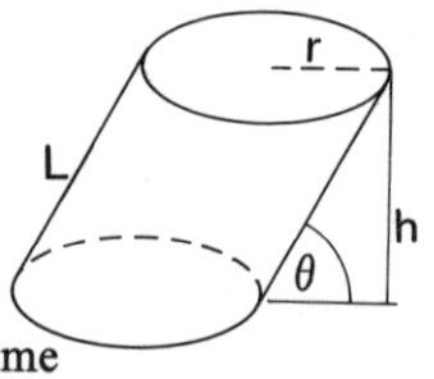

Volume $= \pi r^2 h = \pi r^2 L \sin\theta$

r ☒ ☐ ☒ h ☒ 3.1415927 ☐   RTR: Volume
r ☒ ☐ ☒ 3.1415927 ☒ L ☒ $\sin\theta$ ☐   RTR: Volume

Lateral surface area $= 2\pi r L = \dfrac{2\pi r h}{\sin\theta}$ $2\pi r h \csc\theta$

r ☒ L ☒ 6.2831853 ☐   RTR: Lateral surface area
r ☒ h ☒ 6.2831853 ⊞ $\sin\theta$ ☐   RTR: Lateral surface area
r ☒ h ☒ 6.2831853 ☒ $\csc\theta$ ☐   RTR: Lateral surface area

Total area $= 2\pi r (L + r)$

L ⊞ r ☒ r ☒ 6.2831853 ☐   RTR: Total area

Spherical Cap

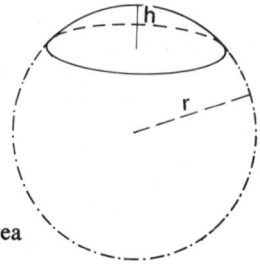

Volume $= \dfrac{\pi h^2 (3r - h)}{3}$

3 ☒ r ⊟ h ☒ h ☒ h ☒ 1.0471976 ☐
   RTR: Volume

Surface area $= 2\pi r h$
r ☒ h ☒ 6.2831853 ☐   RTR: Surface area

Geometric Formulas

Frustrum of Right Circular Cone

$$Volume = \frac{\pi h(a^2 + ab + b^2)}{3}$$

Lateral surface area $= \pi(a + b)\sqrt{h^2 + (b - a)^2}$
$= \pi(a + b)L$

a ⊞ b ⊠ L ⊠ 3.1415927 ⊟
   RTR: Lateral surface area

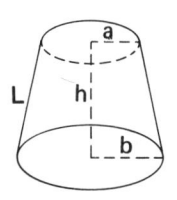

Frustrum of Pyramid

$$Volume = \frac{h(a + b + \sqrt{ab})}{3}$$

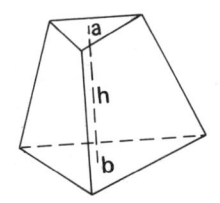

Spherical Triangle of Angles *A, B, C* on Sphere of Radius *r*

(Angles in radians)
Area of triangle $= r^2(A + B + C - \pi)$
A ⊞ B ⊞ C ⊟ 3.1415927 ⊠ r ⊠ r ⊟   RTR: Area of triangle

If the angles are in degrees, then
$A°$ ⊞ $B°$ ⊞ $C°$ ⊟ 180 ⊠ r ⊠ r ⊠ 0.1074533 ⊟   RTR: Area of triangle

Torus

$$Volume = \frac{\pi^2(a + b)(b - a)^2}{4}$$

Surface area $= \pi^2(b^2 - a^2)$

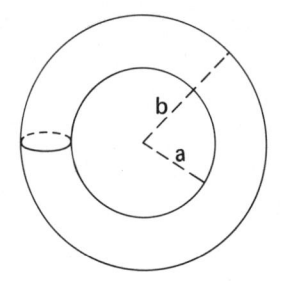

Ellipsoid

$$Volume = \frac{4\pi abc}{3}$$

a ☒ b ☒ c ☒ 4.1887902 ▭   RTR: Volume

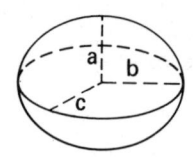

Paraboloid of Revolution

$$Volume = \frac{\pi b^2 a}{2}$$

b ☒ ▭ ☒ a ☒ 1.5707963 ▭   RTR: Volume

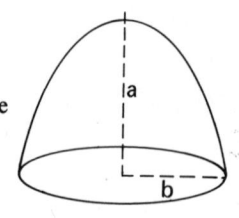

INDEX

Abbreviations vii
Abscissa 89
Addition 5, 18, 135
Aggregation 16, 22, 23, 25
Algebraic entry notation 3
Algebraic equation 15, 103
Algebraic logic 3
Algebraic number 18, 24
Algorithm 20
And so on . . . 10, 141
Angle 147
Annuities 77
Arc 148
Area 145
Arithmetic 9, 15
Arrangement 120
Axis (X and Y) 89
Bar of fraction 19
Base of exponent or radical 20
Base of percentage 39
Binomial formula 139
Braces 23, 141
Brackets 23, 141
Buying price 43
Calculator's features 3
Cap (spherical) 151
Capital 61, 67, 74, 77
Car performance 35

Chain calculation 6, 18, 24, 28
Circle 148
Circumference 147
Combination
  (simple) 120, 124
  (complete) 120, 124
Coefficient of determination 105, 108
Commercial paper 73
Complex number 10
Compound interest 67
Cone of revolution 149
Constant
  Algebraic 16
  Calculator's 6, 26
  Special 129, 137
Conversion
  Area 53
  Length 51
  Mass 56
  Temperature 57
  Volume 55
Cost 43
Counting number 10
Cylinder 150
Data point 89, 111
Days, number of 63, 74
Decimal 11

153

Decimal fraction 19, 64, 71
Decimal point 5, 129, 135
Definitions 9, 16, 91
Degree 137, 147, 148
Delta 140
Denominator 19, 25
Dependent (/In) (Events) 117
Diagonal 145
Digits (significant) 130
Direct reduction of a loan 77
Discount 48
Discount to yield 73
Dividend 19
Division 5, 19, 28, 134
Divisor 19, 134
Dow Jones Industrial Average 90
Ellipse 148
Ellipsoid 152
Empty set 10
Entry of a number 5
Equal sign key 4
Event (future) 115, 125
Exclusive (events) 117
Expectation 117
Exponent 7, 20, 133
Exponential notation 129
Extremes 34
Factor 19, 23, 26
  special 139
Factorial 12, 120, 141
Fit 105, 107, 110
Formula 16
Formulas
  annuities 77
  arithmetic mean 85
  coefficient of determination 108
  combination–
    simple 124
    complete 125
  compound interest 71
  conversion–(area) 53, (length)
    51, (mass) 56, (temperature)
    57, (volume) 55
  discount 48
  discount ot yield 74
  expectation 117
  geometric mean 86
  geometry–(plane) 145, (solid)
    149

harmonic mean 87
markup 43
multiple trade discount 49
orbital speed of a planet 17
percentages 39
permutation 120, (of objects not
  all different) 121, 122
probability–(dependent events)
  119, (exclusive events) 118,
  (independent events) 119,
  (nonexclusive events) 118, (of
  failure) 116, (that an event
  will happen exactly "k" times)
  125
restructuring of 27
series–(arithmetic) 143,
  (geometric) 144, (infinite)
  144
simple interest 64
special -s 138
straight line 92
trend line 99
variation–(complete) 123,
  (simple) 122
Four-registers stack 25
Fraction 19, 26, 129
Fractional number 9
Frequency 88
Frustrum 67
Function 3, 18
  key 4
  symbols 18
Future value 61, 68, 74, 78
Generalized steps
  annuities 78
  arithmetic mean 85
  coefficient of determination 108
  compound interest 71
    when "n" = integer 69
  conversions–(area) 53, (length)
    51, (mass) 56, (temperature)
    57, (volume) 55
  discount to yield 74
  geometric mean 86
  geometry–(plane) 145, (solid)
    149
  harmonic mean 87
  linear regression 105
  markup 43

Index

multiple trade discount 50
percentage 41
power—raising to a 8
reciprocal 12
restructuring of formulas 27
root calculation 21
simple interest 64
Graph 90, 107
Greek alphabet 140
Hypothenuse 146
Imaginary number 10, 23, 139
Index of radical 20
Infinity 141
Integer 9, 20, 68
Integral 141
Integral part 74
Interest 61, 68
Interest rate 61, 68, 74, 77
Intermediate result 25
Inverse 20
Irrational number 9
Iterative solution 20
Least squares method 89
Limit 141
Linear regression 89, 105
Logarithm 20
Margin 43
Markup 43
Mathematical formula 15
Mean
  arithmetic 85, 109
  geometric 86
  harmonic 87
Means 34
Median 88
Memory 25, 99
Metric prefixes 136
Mode 88
Multiple trade discount 48
Multiplication 5, 19, 28, 133
Natural number 10, 22
Negative integer 10
Number entry keys 4
Numerator 19, 25
Numerical system (U.S. & French) 136
Operations 5, 133
Orbital speed of the earth 17
Ordinate 89

Overflow 18, 26
Paraboloid 152
Parallelepiped 149
Parallelogram 146
Parentheses 22, 27, 141
Payment 77
Percent 39, 47, 61, 141
Percentage 39, 46, 61
Perimeter 146
Period 61, 68, 74, 81
Permutation 120
Pi (π) 13, 17, 137
Polygon 147
Positive integer 10, 140
Power, Number raised to a 7, 20, 130
Prefix sign 23
Present value 61, 68, 74, 81
Principal 61, 67, 74, 77
Probability of success 116
Probability of failure 116
Probability 115, 125
  composed 117
  simple 116
Product 19, 22, 141
  Of a series 13, 141
  Special 139
Proportion 34, 35
  (Solution by the) 34, 36
Pyramid 149
Quotient 19, 22
Radian 137, 148
Radical 20, 141
Radicand 20
Rate 39, 47, 48, 61, 68, 74, 77
Ratio 36
Rational number 9, 19
Real number 9, 23, 86, 139
Reciprocal 12, 28, 130
Rectangle 145
Rectangular Cartesian coordinates system 90
Reduction to the unit, Solution by 35, 37, 39
Relation 33
Repetitive decimal 11
Restructuring 18, 26
Reverse Polish Notation 3, 25
Root (s) 20, 21, 23, 139

Rule of signs 23
Rule of three 33, 39
Scales 89
Scientific notation 129
Sector 148
Segment 148
Selling price 43
Semiperimeter 146
Series 86, 88, 143
  arithmetic 143
  geometric 144
  infinite 144
Sigma (Σ) 13, 99, 109, 140
Signs 23
Simple interest 61
Sinking fund 77
Slope 92, 103
Speed of light 129
Sphere 150
Square 145
Step−Saving 25
Stock price 19
Straight line, equation of 92
Subscript 11
Subtraction 5, 19, 135
Summation 13, 99
Symbols 18, 141
Symbols of relationship 10
Tangent 94
Tax (income & sales) 42

Term (algebraic) 22, 135, 143
Time 61, 74, 90
Torus 152
Trapezoid 147
Trend line 89, 96, 105
Triangle 146
  equilateral 146
  plane 146
  right 146
  spherical 152
Unknown 16, 33
Variable 16
Variation
  complete 120, 122
  simple 120, 122
Variation
  direct 33, 36, 62
  inverse 33, 36
Volume 149
Y−Intercept 92
Y(projected) 97
Year
  commercial 63
  business 63
  civil 63
  calendar 63
  fraction of 62
  number of 61, 68
Zero 10, 129